The Secrets To University

From a Student's Experience

The Secrets To University

From a Student's Experience

Stephen Smith

KPH

First Edition 2010
The Key Publishing House Inc.
Toronto, Canada
Website: www. thekeypublish. com
E-mail: info@thekeypublish. com
ISBN 978-0-9811606-4-1 e-Book

Cover Design Alexa Simmons
Proof reading and copyediting Jennifer South
Typesetting Velin Saramov

Library and Archives Canada Cataloguing in Publication

Smith, Stephen,
    The secrets to university : from a student's experience / Stephen Smith.

ISBN 978-0-9811606-4-1

    1. College student orientation--Canada--Handbooks, manuals, etc.
2. College students--Canada--Life skills guides. 3. Study skills--
Handbooks, manuals, etc. 4. Smith, Stephen, 1989-. I. Title.

LB2343.34.C3S63 2010   378.1'980971   C2009-906401-4

Printed and bound in USA. This book is printed on paper suitable for recycling and made from fully sustained forest sources.

Published by a grant and in association with The Key Research Center (www. thekeyresearch. org). The Key promotes freedom of thought and expression and peaceful coexistence among human societies.

KPH

Table of Contents

Chapter One

Hello, and Welcome!

Hello, and welcome! You've decided to embark on one of life's great journeys: university. I wrote this book to help you get through it as easily as possible, hopefully more easily than I did. Why should you read my book as opposed to the hundreds of other university prep books out there? You should read it because I have the best experience.

Think about it—would you trust a medical textbook that wasn't written by a doctor? Or one written by a doctor who hadn't set foot in a hospital in twenty years? I don't think so. So why would you want the advice of someone whose memories of what university is really like have long since faded?

I was in your position not too long ago, looking for any advice I could get about what university would be like. But when I walked through the bookstore, all the books were written by people who looked like my parents. And if you're anything like me, your parents have already given you enough advice. I lived through first year university just like those authors did, but I did it last year. You want advice about what university is like right now, as opposed to what it used to be like, right?

And that's why I wrote this book—to give you insight about what university is like right now, this year. You'll learn about things that no university pamphlet will have, and things that no information lecture or "Open House" will cover. You'll also learn about the things that universities do cover, but for some reason nobody uses.

Note: For simplicity's sake, I am going to be assuming that you are going to a university and that your program will last four years. I understand that some programs last two, and that in the U.S., they prefer calling it college rather than university. But I also assume that if you're smart enough to get into any sort of post-secondary education program, you're smart enough to make the change in your head. Thanks!

You'll hear about what my first year was like, and I won't spare any detail. You'll hear about how it started out great, took a gigantic nosedive, and then you'll hear about what I did to get it back. There are things you can do every month to succeed in university, and I'll tell you what they are. We'll delve into more detail later on, but first I'll tell you about how I got to this point.

In high school, I was shy, nerdy, and introspective. For the first ten years of my schooling, I kept to myself largely, did my work, and had few friends. And then, in the span of a few months, all of my friends except one moved away, for various reasons. My world collapsed, and the next year was pretty lonely.

However, it gave me a lot of time to think, and I'm thankful for that. I believe that the silver lining of becoming a total social outcast overnight was that I was able to sit back and really think, "Who am I? Who do I want to be? How am I going to get there?" I thought about what made me the happiest, what I'd had the most fun doing. My mind drifted back two years, to when my friends and I had entered a provincial video competition, creating advertisements for a fictional product of our own devising.

We were given a video camera, and allowed to run free over the school. I remember leaving class to film (with school sanction of course—I was still a nerd, I would never cut class without permission), and having the time of my life. I decided that Marketing was the industry for me. But this lead to an inexorable conclusion—when was the last time you saw a successful marketing professional who's also cripplingly shy?

I'm still nerdy and introspective, I wouldn't be writing this book if I weren't. But I decided that the shyness had to go. I read up on methods of meeting new people and ran into a technique from, surprisingly, the world of marketing. It was called the "reciprocal effect", and it basically states that if you do something to someone, they will feel like doing the same to you.

This is used in marketing through the offering of free samples—they give you something, you feel like you want to do something for them in return. And oh look, here they are suggesting exactly what you can do to pay them back—buy their product!

I decided that I would try to apply the reciprocal effect to my life, except in a more benevolent fashion. I would be friendly to people, even people I didn't know, and see what would happen. Hopefully people would start to notice me. I couldn't in my wildest dreams have imagined what happened next. It worked! People started being friendly back. Practicing simple acts of kindness like smiling at somebody, or waving and saying "Hello!" to a stranger had turned my social situation around entirely, and I couldn't be happier.

Off of this momentum, I enrolled in a class called Leadership 12. It was a course that was supposed to teach you how to be a better leader, and I wondered how they planned to do this in a classroom setting. They told me on my first day that it would be experiential. I soon found out that that meant, "You're going to do public speaking every day for an entire semester". That terrified me, as it would most people, I'm sure. But I stuck with it, I did public speaking every day, and I became very, very good at it. It's now one of my favourite things to do, amazingly.

In Grade Twelve, I ran for Valedictorian of my graduating class. It was an elected position, as opposed to just having the person with the best grades do it. There were ten candidates, so an additional level of screening was introduced: we were required to take a sixty second snippet out of our speech, stand up in front of over three hundred people (I went to a decently-sized high school), and talk. It was one of the most exhilarating days of my life.

After all the speeches were made, votes were cast for the four candidates who would make it to the final round. I was one of the four. This meant that I had to go before a panel of staff (and a camera), and give my entire speech. I did so, and they went with someone else, but I was still proud that I had conquered my demons of shyness. And now the future lay ahead. What would I do?

I wanted to go somewhere with an excellent business program, and lucky me, I had the best undergraduate business program in Canada right on my doorstep: the Sobey School of Business, a part of Saint Mary's University. As you may have already done, I attended Open Houses and Information Sessions and various other things designed to brainwash me into joining them. And it worked.

Now that I knew where I was going, I engaged two major parts of my personality: obsessive research, and a penchant for looking too far into the future. I spent the next few months reading everything I could get with the word "University" on it, and designing how perfect my life would be this coming September. My family held a going away party for me, and I was sure that everything was going to turn out great. And then September actually came.

The first few days were great, actually. I moved into my residence room, met my new roommate, and got generally settled in to what my new reality was like. Frosh Week was great. My university held events like a Casino Night, BBQs and a formal dinner, and those were entertaining.

An event called Turfburn was, and still is, a campus tradition. You spend an afternoon on the Saint Mary's turf bonding with fellow first-year students and getting a sunburn (hence the name). At the time, though, I thought it was called Turfburn because of my shredded knees—artificial turf and bare skin don't play well together. At night, a Joel Plaskett concert rocked the campus. I was as happy as could be.

But then I hit a wall, and I crashed so hard and so deep that I didn't come up for air until Thanksgiving. I skipped the rest of Frosh Week, preferring to sleep all day instead.

The next few weeks were among the worst I've ever experienced in my life. I was a mess—I was constantly nauseous, I was often shivering despite the fact that it was September, and I started to experience paranoid delusions. I'd be in the shower, and suddenly be struck with a paralyzing fear that while I was in the shower, everyone I knew in the outside world had died. I would call home five times a day, driving my parents insane with my tearful jabbering.

I'd come home every chance I got, and crash on my bed to sleep, only waking when it was time to go back to school. I bought a locker to store my things in, just in case it got to the point that I couldn't stand it any more, and had to drop out of residence. It was my insurance policy, and it made me feel better knowing it was there. I lost interest in things I used to love, and took to sleeping all day in my room. Or at least trying to.

I couldn't even sleep, I was too nervous. I diagnosed myself with every illness known to man, from General Anxiety Disorder to Obsessive Compulsive Disorder to depression to "maybe I'm just insane". I was slowly reverting back to the shy version of myself. I didn't want to, but I didn't know how to stop.

Looking back on it now it seems like madness, but it truly had a grip on me, and wasn't letting go any time soon. What had happened to transform me from a smiling high school student to a mentally barren possible university drop-out? And how could I reverse it?

University is a tough adjustment. Any sociology major (and you'll meet quite a few) will tell you that when you take someone out of their accustomed environment and place them in a totally new one, there's bound to be some transitional uneasiness. Of course, they're usually referring to the behaviours prisoners exhibit during their first period of incarceration. University isn't that bad, but the theory still holds.

Part of my problem was that I was having trouble fitting in. Or rather, my brain had convinced me that I was having trouble fitting in. Looking back now, I was doing fine, meeting new people and forging new bonds. But my brain, addled with sleep deprivation and a nervous displacement, wasn't quite reading reality at that point.

Another big problem was my double room. I'm sure you can relate to the fact that I like my privacy at times. It's great to be around people, but not all the time, right? Everyone needs to have a place where they can be alone, lock the door, and chill by themselves. And since I had a roommate, this was taken away from me. That loss of privacy played serious tricks with my mind. It's much harder to cry in bed and call your parents in the middle of the night if someone is five feet away, especially when you're a guy. Just ask that same sociology major, they'll tell you.

I eventually requested a transfer to a single room, that transfer was granted, and it helped a lot, but I still had other problems to deal with. I later discovered that my roommate requested a transfer to a single room about a month after I did. So I guess a corollary lesson here is that no matter what you do, you're not the only one doing it, so don't feel bad.

Another problem was my new classes. Again, looking back at my final grades for that semester, I did fine (straight As), but for those first few weeks my brain was operating in a different universe. I was convinced that I was going to fail all my exams and have to go work minimum wage for the rest of my life. You might experience the same thing, but since you were smart enough to pick up this book, you can help yourself through, and your friends too, if they're struggling.

So now you're thinking, "Wow Steve, you were kind of a total mess, weren't you? How'd you fix it?" Well, it's just one of those "day at a time" things. Keep doing the right things (read: the things that are in this book) and your life will gradually improve. For me personally, I received a tremendous amount of support from my family. When I put out a call, my family rushed to help, giving me tips on how to survive, and anecdotes from their own university days.

I also went to counselling. Yes, I did. And it was amazing. In fact, it helped me out so much that I would encourage anyone who is considering it to do it, especially if your school offers free counsellors like Saint Mary's does. Long story short: if you want to see a counsellor, do it.

Another thing that helped me was involving myself in extra-curricular activities. My university has something called a Random Acts of Kindness team, and I decided to join it. They do things like hand out free candy on Halloween. I don't know if you've ever tried to hand out free candy, but it's deceptively difficult. I guess the students at my university had good parents, and now refuse to take candy from strangers. I also got involved with a group called Fusion Halifax, and met lots of great people.

But some of the best things I got involved with were simple social groups. I joined my university's Commerce Society, which took me all across the city to places I'd never been and activities I'd never done, despite growing up thirty minutes from the city. My university runs a program called First Year Initiative, or FYI, which acts as a support group for first-year students. Some of the people I met in that group are now my closest friends, and I learned how to slowly restore myself to what I once was. It was a good feeling.

I also joined the Marketing Society. As I said before, I love Marketing, it's my passion. If anyone out there is hiring, call me. But back to my present job, writing this book. My time with the Marketing Society was some of my best time spent that year. The people there were different than normal—they liked me. I didn't have to do anything to convince them, they just liked me for no reason, they liked me because I was me. And that was a good feeling too.

The final thing that helped me was time. It may seem like little help, and that's because it is, but you just have to trust me that if you follow these tips, things will eventually get better. It's inevitable.

But what if you don't have access to these things? As sad as it may seem, some people don't have supportive parents, or their university doesn't recognize the importance of peer support and professional counselling. You can still make it through. The main battle is inside, that's what's important. If you can follow this book by yourself, and hold on until things improve, you'll make it. I believe in you, however corny that may sound.

Eventually, Thanksgiving rolled around. I had quite a bit to be thankful for. I felt like things were getting better, I was finally getting to the light at the end of the tunnel. Seeing my family and friends again re-energized me to take another shot at life. I hit a bit of a wall right after the weekend, but I was able to push through. Thanksgiving was also the first time I was able to really sit down and consider my year so far.

I thought that other people might benefit from my experience, so like any good university student, I wrote about it on Facebook. I've attached that original writing as an appendix to this book.

Saint Mary's has always had a very strong varsity sports program, and the most popular sport is football. So when our team made it to the Vanier Cup, Canada's national championship for university football, I knew I had to go. The tickets were due to go on sale the morning after a Commerce Society event, and I decided to camp out outside the Student Centre overnight to assure I would get a ticket. I dressed up in every warm article of clothing I could find, and it was a good time. I got a ticket, and the trip was later that week.

We gathered outside the Student Centre, and CBC had decided to show up and interview us about our Saint Mary's passion. We attempted to restrict the amount of vulgar insults directed against the other team, but some emerged anyway. On the twenty-four hour bus ride there, we watched a total of twelve movies, five with Vince Vaughn, and three with Will Ferrell. We stopped at several Irving locations, and it began to be a game noting the similarities in the locations.

We drove through a snowstorm, strong enough that I couldn't see the road outside my window. At one point, we parked in Kingston, Ontario, and discovered a place with gas stations on all four corners of its intersection. When we finally arrived in Toronto, we had freedom to explore until the game started that night, and I had a great time. Saint Mary's would eventually lose the game, but I still count the trip as a success. However, my twenty-four hours back to Halifax were marked by a stark realization: your parents can embarrass you anywhere, even when you're halfway across the country.

What motivated this realization? My parents had insisted that I continuously call in and check with them, and I thought I had been complying with this. I had called my mother's workplace, and left a voicemail message. On Saturday. Whoops. I had also taken off my jacket (with the cell phone in the pocket) and placed it in the overhead storage bin. Another big mistake. Over the next few hours, my parents began frantically calling the cell phone that I could not hear, and driving themselves insane.

When I did not answer, they became even more frantic, and called the Halifax police. The Halifax police referred them to the Ontario Provincial Police, who referred them to the tour bus company, who called the individual bus I was riding on. At the next rest stop, an announcement was made to the entire bus (including many of my newfound friends): "Is there a Stephen Smith on this bus?" "Yes." "Call your mother, she's worried about you." And that's when I realized that parental embarrassment transcends time and space.

After that trip of a lifetime, there was still the matter of my first set of exams to write. I wrote four exams in five days, and had a fifth a week later. Exam periods are interesting because they basically boil down to this: "OK, you only have class for five days out of seventeen, an hour or two each day, but what you do on those days will determine 30-60 percent of your mark. Sound good?" So they can be some of the most free times of your year, or they can very tough. Here's hoping you get the first one.

After exams comes Christmas vacation. It truly is the most wonderful time of the year, as it's impossible for you to have any readings or assignments or projects to do. It's also likely the first time you'll be home for an extended period, so be ready for another shock. Remember, transferring from one environment to another always comes with some shock, but hopefully going from university to home will be easier than the other way around.

I remember tearing up as I was leaving my residence room with my father, saying, "I never thought I'd make it this far. I never thought I'd pack a suitcase, leave here, lock the door, and still intend to come back." It was a powerful moment, one that made the past four months all worthwhile. And it was worthwhile.

Coming back for second semester, I was nervous once more. My counselling had finished just before the break, and so had FYI. Was I ready to stand on my own, with no support net? Turns out there were two answers: I was ready, but I also had a support net that I had completely forgotten about: the people I'd met in first semester. They were back too, and it wasn't long before I was laughing and chatting and trading Christmas stories with them.

If there's one cycle I kept repeating over and over during my first year, it's that of unwarranted worry, followed by wondering, "Why did I ever worry about that?" These days I've tried to see when I'm falling into old habits, but I still do it occasionally. Like I've said, if you can't eliminate a habit, try to at least reduce it to get some benefit.

Another part of my personality is that I do odd things when I'm bored. Like write books. In February 2008, I decided that taking my friend and visiting all twenty-six Tim Hortons locations on the Halifax peninsula in one day was a good idea. I made a map, my friend (who has serious graphic design skills for a Physics/Chemistry major) made a logo that said *TimQuest 2008*, and we were off. A few months later, he said, "Steve, the only reason I came along with you on that trip was that I thought if you did it alone you would die."

Despite his objections, I had an excellent time, and we received quite a bit of media coverage for our little stunt. We were mentioned on Z103.5, a local radio station, we were filmed for "The 'fax", a local television show, and we were interviewed for the Halifax Daily News. The Daily News put us front and centre, with a large picture of the two of us and a nearly full page story. I always thought that we would get some coverage, but I never imagined just how big it would be.

Along the way on our twelve hour odyssey, we ran into Tim Hortons employees who gave us free food because they'd heard of us, people who wanted pictures with us, and people who wanted to sign our shirts. We were both nearly run down by cars in parking lots. I always thought that TimQuest might end with me in the hospital, but being run over by a car wasn't the way I thought it might happen.

Some notes from the trip:

- I met my instructor from FYI, and she seemed overjoyed at my improvement from September.
- Despite the trek taking place in February, I was still able to purchase a "Candy Cane Donut" at one remotely-located Tim Hortons.
- I eventually felt the effect of what I'd later discover is called "caffeine intoxication".
- Speaking of intoxication, I met a group of people in their forties, going to a Michael Bublé concert that was on that night, who were all totally obliterated. I didn't see that coming.

By the end of the day, I could barely move, I was oversugared and overcaffeinated, simultaneously tired and hyper. And it was worth it.

I also set up a website so that our adoring fans (read: my family and Nick's family) could track our progress and see how it turned out. But thanks to the media coverage we received, thousands of people flocked to the page during the week of our trip, and the month after. If there's anything I learned from TimQuest, it's that the only way to get what you want is to ask. Just ask, and you'll be surprised at the results.

Every year, my university holds a "Battle of the Floors" day of competition, it's kind of like a Residence Olympics. Some people say that it's not the destination that's interesting, it's the journey. My journey to Battle of the Floors was certainly interesting. So interesting that I've changed the names of the people involved.

I woke up the morning of Battle of the Floors, and tried to get to the washroom. I found I couldn't do this, as Joe was sitting in a chair, blocking the middle of the hall. I asked him, "Joe, why are you sitting in a chair in the hall?" He said, "I screwed up my ankle, man." Apparently he had fallen on some ice running for a cab and not noticed the pain until waking up the next morning.

I asked, "Does anyone have crutches in their room?", and luck of luck, someone did. When asked why they had a pair of crutches just lying around, they said that it was because of chronic knee problems.

So we taped Joe up and got him on crutches, then went to wake up Moe, one of the other guys living on my floor. When we went into their section of the floor, I noticed that one of the couches from our lounge was in the hall. I asked, "Why is there a couch in the hall?" and was told, "Because they moved it out of Moe's room". I didn't think to ask, "Why was it in Moe's room?"

We walked by the washroom, and inside there was a toilet with no seat, and a shower with no curtain. I made the mistake of asking, "Why?" once again. According to Joe, Moe had had a few too many last night, and ripped the toilet seat off while trying to get away from two people who were attempting to force him to vomit "for his own good". So that's where the toilet seat went, but what about the shower curtain? Allegedly, Moe had charged at the men, and ended up ripping the shower curtain down as he missed.

Also in the washroom was a pile of paper about two feet high and three feet across. It was the entire phone book, separated into individual pages and stacked in a pile. I asked once again, "Why?", and was told that it had also come out of Moe's room. This time, I had the presence of mind to ask, "Why was it in Moe's room?" and was met with, "Because we stuffed it under his door page by page while he was passed out." I decided not to go any further, and ask why they did that. We finally got to Moe's room, and he was apparently still feeling the effects of last night.

I've asked people if they've ever woken up still drunk, and apparently it's pretty common (even certain members of my family, who shall remain nameless, have admitted to it happening to them "once or twice"). Moe's intoxication was presumably caused by the fact that he had consumed a large part of a bottle of Jagermeister in the form of Jagerbombs the previous night. This had evidently had a considerable effect on his mental stability, and as I was about to find out, his bladder.

We knocked on his door. We heard him stagger up, the rustle of a shirt being put on, a scream, and a fall on the floor. Upon entering his room, we noticed that the shirt he had attempted to put on was soaked in his own urine, along with his bed. This was met by much mocking and derision by my companions.

Long story short? We were wrecked, all of us. Some of us were extremely fatigued, some of us were still drunk from last night, and some of us were on crutches. All in all, we were a good team. We finally made it to the event, and once Joe had gotten a seat and some ice for his ankle, he relinquished his crutches to Moe, who frankly needed them more at this point. The actual event was a fun time, but it simply couldn't compete with the trip getting there.

I also entered the First Annual Hamachi Group Business Competition. The Hamachi Group is a set of restaurants in Halifax, and they knew that if they wanted smart business students, they should come to Saint Mary's. I recruited Stephanie Pronk, another friend of mine, and together we entered the contest. Luckily, the people at Hamachi felt that we couldn't analyze their business without spending an evening there, so they gave us a seventy-five dollar gift certificate to one of their restaurants.

Now I just had to convince Stephanie's boyfriend at the time that it was a requirement of the competition for me to take his girlfriend out to dinner. The three of us had been friends for years, and he knew I loved business far more than girlfriend poaching, so he was very understanding about it. It was a lovely time, and then came the easy part—writing a consulting report. They must have liked what they saw, as we won second place, despite competing against teams of third and fourth year students! I was immensely happy.

After that, I wrote my second set of exams, and that was it. I was through it, and alive. My second year has been even better than my first year—I was elected President of the Marketing Society, and my success in the Hamachi Competition led to an invitation to be on the Saint Mary's team for the Intercollegiate Business Competition (ICBC). I started getting involved with Advancing Canadian Entrepreneurship (ACE), and served as the Marketing Director of the Saint Mary's University Environmental Society (SMUES). I have more acronyms than I know what to do with, and it's great.

So let's sum up—my year started off down in the depths of university Hades, then it started to very slowly get better, then it started to get quite a bit better, then it started to get really good, and right now it's pretty fantastic. By picking up this book, you've shown that you have the same initiative to be successful. Now let's go through your first year in more detail.

Chapter Two

Frosh Week Fun

A lright, so this book is going to be a journey, just like university. Except that we're actually going to start before the beginning, while you're still in high school. Depending on your family's penchant for moving, you may have gone to school with some of these people your whole life, and know them very well. Your teachers are consistent, and the work is, honestly, not that bad. It's a calming place, a place you know, a place you've spent time in.

Or maybe it's your version of hell on earth, and you can't wait to walk out those doors once and for all. Everyone's high school experience is different, and a lot of people would rather just forget the whole ordeal and focus on the future. So that's what we'll do—don't look back, eyes on the road ahead. And what's ahead? Well, that's really your decision.

Some people will decide to jump into the workforce right away, either as entrepreneurs or due to financial constraints. This is a fine choice, but I'd like to throw a statistic your way: according to Forbes, a person with a university degree makes, on average, TWICE as much as a person without one. In addition, they also have lower levels of unemployment.

Now I hear what you're saying. But what about Bill Gates, Steve? He didn't go to university, and now he has enough money that he could swim in a pool of it, if it wouldn't be massively uncomfortable and give him multiple paper cuts. This is partially true. But it needs some correction:

1. Bill Gates went to university, he just decided to drop out later.
2. The university that he dropped out of was Harvard.
3. He dropped out because he already had a business that was making money.

Let's examine these points for a second. Dropping out of university is not what made Bill Gates rich. Working on computers in high school, getting into Harvard, meeting his future business partner Steve Ballmer there, and then founding a business that was so massively successful he had to drop out is what made Bill Gates rich. Maybe. Microsoft could have just as easily been a massive failure, and he'd have passed up the chance to get a world-class education. The decision of whether to go to university or not is a personal one, and one that you should spend a considerable amount of time pondering on.

Done? Already? I guess that since you're reading this book, you've probably already made the decision that you're going to university. But where? And for what? The questions just keep coming. But they're both important things to think about. I will tell you right now that if you answer "whatever my high school friends are doing" or "whatever my parents want" to those questions, you're going to regret it fairly quickly.

This is a theme I'll likely keep coming back to in the book: individuality. You are your own person, with your own brain, and your own interests. Making an investment of the next four years of your life is something that only you can decide on. So choose well. Luckily, you've made the wise choice of buying this book, so I'm here to help you.

First off, the question of where to go. It's a simple choice that will define your life for the next few years, so it's best if you give it a bit of thought. In fact, why don't you think on it while we move on to the second step, i.e. what you're going to study. See, this is the problem most students face: they feel they have to choose a place to go, and then a program that that institution offers. That's completely backwards.

Think about it—if you were buying a car, which one of these things would you do first?

1. Decide which dealership to go to
2. Decide what kind of car you want

See what I mean? They're both important choices, but one is clearly something you should do first, before you do the other. So what is it that you want to do? It's the question of a lifetime, really. An institution defines you for four years, but your career is with you for life (hopefully). How you decide this comes back to another one of this book's central tenets: introspection. Nobody knows you better than you, so you should be the first person you ask when you have a question about yourself.

I talk to a lot of my friends, and a lot of them aren't sure what they want to do with their life. If you've picked up this book, chances are you fall into one of two piles: you're either a hyperintelligent go-getter who sees university as another challenge to be conquered, and wants the best information available in order to make things easy, or you're....normal. Normal people don't always know what they want, but they want to know what they want. So that's what this book is for—to help you think on that. It's jampacked full of information for our megageniuses in the corner over there, but also stuffed with tips on how to figure out just what to do with your life now that your high school doesn't expect you to show up in September.

Think back. Back to the happiest you ever were. Now ask yourself the following questions, and write down the answers.

• What were you doing?
• What about this particular time made it great?
• How could you make money from doing that every day?

I sort of did this already, back in my introduction. Due to a period of unexpected loneliness, I was forced to really examine my life, and think back to all the good times I'd had. I then started going through them, and asking myself what about them made them spectacular.

• During my best times, what was I doing?
 o Creating
• What about creating made it great?
 o Freedom
• How could I make money from doing that every day?
 o Start my own company

Now obviously I don't expect everyone reading this book to start their own company. If you do, then who am I going to hire? What I'm saying is that by following this three-step process, you can come a whole lot closer to what you were put on this earth to do.

And that's really what it comes down to: You are here. You are incredible. What are you going to do about it? What do you want to do to make people notice you? What are you, as a unique human being, going to offer the world that will make people stop and stare in wonder? When you answer those questions you have a career.

So, you've gone through the forest, either metaphorically or possibly literally (camping is a lot of fun, and a good way to clear your head), and you have a fairly good idea of what you want to do with your life. The next step is to accept that you might be wrong.

I know, it it's tough to spend all that time thinking about life and existence and all those other concepts you're going to pretend to understand when your Philosophy prof asks you to write a paper on them, but the fact remains that you may get to university and completely change your mind as to what your higher purpose is. That's why it's important to choose a good university. I'll come back to the car analogy again: imagine you've done all your research, picked out the perfect car, go to the dealership, and oh no! The car doesn't have enough cup holders! You need at least seven, and it only has six.

This is where a good dealership comes in, as they can show you other cars that are similar to the one you had originally liked, but with more cup holders. And luckily, this choice, while not being any easier to make, is at least easier to research: universities want your money. Badly. They will come to you personally if they think it will help them get it.

And that's where your high school's university fair comes in! Choosing a career was tough, because careers don't have marketing departments. Universities, however, do. Depending on when you read this, you may have already seen one: your high school gym plastered in the school colours of fifty different schools, over-peppy university fanboys and fangirls proselytizing about the values of their institutions, and lots and lots of free swag.

Hopefully, your high school will let you know what places are coming, and you can read up on them a little bit beforehand. If not, don't worry about it, the reps will be more than happy to tell you all about the place paying them to talk to you. However, if you want to at least look like you did your homework, try to steer away from questions that have a blatantly obvious answer. It's the harsh truth, but there is such a thing as a stupid question. Would you go to Starbucks and ask if they serve coffee?

However, there is an exception. If there's a question that's answered in the brochure, but could be better answered by a human, ask away! For example, a brochure can tell you where the school is located, but a student there can tell you what places are nearby. The website might say what programs are offered, but a student can tell you which ones are the most popular. And so on.

I could put a list of sample questions here for you to ask, but I've been at enough events to tell when someone is asking questions that they memorized because they thought they were supposed to, rather than ones that they actually want to know the answer to. Ask about the programs they offer, what their admission requirements are, what a typical day would be like, anything relating to the day to a day in the life of a student.

These universities often offer guided tours of their campuses, which will give you a sense of the campus' feel, and what it would be like to walk back and forth across the grounds a hundred times a day for the next four years. They also offer Open Houses, which are usually day-long events with free food and speeches and other promotional flappery.

They're both great events, and will help you make your decision, but once again it has to come down to some serious thinking about what you want to do with your life, and which institution will most help you do that. No amount of bouncy castles and barbecues can make up for substandard teaching facilities.

So you've chosen a university, you apply, they accept you, and life is glorious! Oh what a happy day. Now let's fast forward a little bit, to the point where you actually have to attend the place.

So the big day has arrived. Time to move in. If your university is smart, they'll have spread it over a few days, to avoid a massive crush of people. I would suggest renting a cart from U-Haul or a similar place, rather than relying on the ones the university provides. They can be a bit tough to wrangle, not to mention being in short supply.

Once you're entirely moved in, everything is in its right place, and you're chilling on your new bed, take time to give your parents a call. They're worried about you, and fear that you've somehow managed to screw up eighteen years of their parenting within the first eighteen minutes of you not being around them. So take a minute or two, reassure them, they'll feel better for it.

If you don't call them, they'll call you. And you don't want that, trust me. Do I need to remind you of the Vanier Cup story I told back in Chapter One? The future PR majors reading this book know that it's easier to control the story than have the story control you.

Now you have to buy your textbooks. Now if you've been in a normal bookstore before in your life, you might think that you know how much a book should cost. You would be sadly mistaken. And not only are they alarmingly expensive ($100 on average), but the lineups can be astonishingly long. Luckily, this book will help you defeat both problems, and then some.

First, the cost. The easiest way I've seen to deal with this is simply get there early. Oftentimes, bookstores will buy back books at the end of the semester, slap a "Used" sticker on them, and then sell them to the next crowd of eager students. These sales happen in April, so if you come to the bookstore early, maybe before you even move in, then you have the best chance of snagging some cheap deals.

And of course, you might find yourself on the other end of this equation. I can't tell you the amount of times I've had a course that I could not wait to be over with, and scrub every remnant of it out of my life. It was like a bad relationship or something, these courses. Now if this were a person, you might sell the stuff they forgot to take with them when they moved out. In this case, I was able to sell back the textbooks for the courses, and put the money towards new books. Check out this flow:

1. Buy textbook for $100
2. Sell back for $50
3. Buy new used textbook for $75
4. Total extra cost of second textbook = $25!

It's a great strategy—the bookstore gets extra money, you get a cheap book, everyone wins! But if other things come up, and you can't get to the bookstore early, don't despair, there are other options.

Check to see if your prof has free copies to give away—sometimes the publishers send an extra copy or two as a "thank you for forcing your students to buy our book" present.

Or maybe your student association runs a book exchange where students sell books to students. As a last resort, which is odd because it requires the most lead time, you can consider ordering your books online. Places like Amazon.com and Chegg.com offer cheap textbooks with a catch—you need to factor in time for shipping. So shop around, do your research, find what's best for you.

And the lineups. While these can also be avoided by the whole "show up early" strategy, I never really did that in my first year. But what you will do in your first year is have far, far, far too much reading to catch up on. So why not read your textbook? You might not know which chapters have been assigned, but it's a pretty safe bet that they'll want you to read the first one. By doing this you not only get ahead of the game academically, but you also keep yourself entertained in line.

Back to residence. It's great. Freedom, space, you can do whatever you want. The only thing is that there's another guy/girl living two feet away from you, with just as much freedom to do whatever they want, and the walls are very thin. So how do you manage this situation? Enter the Residence Assistant (known as a "Don" at some institutions).

First off, don't forget that they're a student too. They have classes and exams just like you do, and they're not always perfect. They are there for two main reasons—first, to be a liaison between the university and you, and second, to make sure nobody hosts keg parties at 4 am on a Tuesday and calm you down so you don't murder your roommate when he takes the last cup of coffee without asking you. Both roles are key.

Here is something very important: your RA is in no way required to be your friend. In fact, that is the largest single understanding I came to during my first year of university: **nobody is required to be your friend.** I don't see that as harsh—to me, it just means that the friends I do have are more genuine.

It also means that you should not come to university with pre-existing notions of what your life will be like, because you will likely be wrong. You will make friends at the speed appropriate for you, no matter what your university might say about "oh, you're sure to meet friends at (event name)." They say that for two reasons:

1. It makes you feel better.
2. They're usually right (but not always).

I've been to events where I expected to meet a new best friend, and not met anyone. I've been to events where I thought I would be alone, and met great people. And of course, I've been to places I thought I would meet people, and I did, and I've been to places I thought I would be lonely, and I was. The key is reasonable expectations, and a willingness to have an open mind.

Your RA is not a paramedic, not an ambulance driver, and even if they're a Psych major, they are not licenced to psychoanalyze you. That's what your school's professional counselors are for. However, they are also a human being, so you have every right to expect some basic decency from them. If they're the ones hosting keg parties at 4 am on a Tuesday, that's not right either.

So now that we're a few days into your new university life, why not give your parents another call? Despite your first call, they are likely still worried. Tell them about your textbooks, maybe put them on with your RA, just generally put them at ease.

Next up is an activity to put your own self at ease. Take your schedule, print it off, and go find your classrooms. Not only will it acquaint you with the campus, but it'll make things easier for you when you're stumbling around in the mornings. Who knows—maybe you'll meet someone in the hall, and they'll be in the same class as you, and you'll be able to help them find their way.

There are two main ways one can approach university. One is to come, go to your classes, and leave. The other is to jump into the university experience with both feet, and get your full money's worth with all that your institution has to offer. If you've bought this book, hopefully you're either in the second category or are using this book to help you go there. One of the big things you can do for this is join a society.

I don't want to speak for every university, but at least at Saint Mary's there are a considerable amount of societies, enough that everyone should be able to find at least one that they like. And in the rare occasion that they can't, you can start one! It's a great way to meet people, gain experience, and have a ton of fun doing it.

Another way you can do this is by getting involved in student politics. Whether you know it or not, your student union or student association likely provides a considerable amount of services for students, and they're always looking for new people to join the fun. For example, on my campus, SMU-SA (the Saint Mary's University Students' Association) runs the campus bar, offers a full health and dental plan to students, operates a free late-night shuttle service, and lobbies on a provincial and national level to get student interests represented in government. And that's just a small sample of what's available to students. You also have a say in what goes on—run for President, fill an executive position, or simply volunteer at an event.

Oh, and one last thing. How do they get the money for all of this? From you, in your student fees. So if you're paying for it either way, you may as well use it, right?

If you are a business major, or just like meeting new people, you should consider looking around to see if there are any local networking groups you can join. For example, I joined a group called Fusion Halifax during my first year, and met some amazing people. Similarly, things like volunteering at a local food bank or other charity can be a lot of fun, and on the selfish side, build your resume.

So now we'll skip ahead to your first day of class. You obviously already know where it is, and you've brought something to take notes with, and hopefully you've turned off your cell phone or at least set it to vibrate. One of the major differences between a public high school and university is that the professors are given a bit more leeway in how they deal with students. You're considered to be a big boy or big girl now, so if your prof feels like making a joke at your expense, they probably will. Try your best to not have you cell phone go off in the middle of class, is what I'm saying here. It might not go well for you if it does.

And the note-taking. Another major difference between high school and university is the lecture style. If your high school was anything like mine, you had frequent quizzes, assignments, in-class readings, and other things. In university, the vast majority of your classes will be done in large lecture halls of a few hundred students, where the prof stands at the front with a presentation and simply talks for an hour or two.

Here's a hint: they expect you to listen. And take notes. Some, if not most, of what your prof is saying will be on the final exam, and not a lot of it is in the textbook. However, if you don't read the textbook, you won't have a clue what your prof is saying. So it's important to do both. Read the assigned chapter (or chapters) before you go to class, and take detailed notes while you're there. That's the easiest way to succeed.

How do you balance all these things? At the start of every semester, your prof will hand you a syllabus, in which they'll spell out their plan for the semester—what you'll be reading, when the assignments are due, when the tests are, things like that. Take your day planner, your phone, whatever you're using to stay organized, and write in everything at once.

This way, when you flip over to a new week in two months' time, you can see at a glance what textbook readings you have to do that week, what assignments are due, when you should start reviewing for upcoming tests, and everything you need to know to make sure you stay on top of things. Try setting aside one afternoon a week, say, Monday after classes, to do nothing but textbook reading.

Depending on the prof, there will either be a lot of material from the textbook that you'll be expected to know, none, or somewhere in between. I've had profs where I could literally follow along with my finger in the textbook as they did their lecture. Those profs are ridiculous. I've also had profs who told me "it's your job to read the textbook for theory, come to the lecture if you want to hear how it applies in practice."

Those profs aren't so much ridiculous as rare—not everyone knows their stuff well enough to put together a full set of lectures without touching the textbook once. I once had a Finance prof who would come in every class with nothing but a cup of coffee and a whiteboard marker, and spin the most incredible lectures I have ever had the privilege of enjoying. Oh, how my arm would ache from note-taking after that class. But it was always worth it, for the sheer volume of material that I learned.

And I mean really learned. It was a tough class, but it was an educational class. Not all profs are terrible textbook readers, not all profs are stupendous savants in their fields. The majority of them are simply good at what they do. A good prof mixes a little bit of the textbook with a little bit of personal experience, makes it fairly easy to take notes, covers the major points of the chapters, but expects you to pick up the details on your own. That's what the majority of your profs will be like.

So how do you make the most of your textbook reading time? First, read the chapter. Don't do anything else but read it. Read it intensely—this isn't a magazine, or something light that you can just skim through when you're bored. Think of it like a great work of literature (even if it isn't). Dedicate yourself to understanding the chapters, like you would try to understand the plot in a novel. Of course, sometimes in English classes great works of literature will be your textbooks. Lucky you, then.

By taking one deep pass on it, you pick up the majority of what's in the chapter and lock it away for later. Now you need to take notes for detail. Have a sheet of paper, and while you're reading through it a second time (which should be a day or two after the first time), write down the points that jump out at you as either important or difficult to memorize.

In general, these two categories are what comprise the majority of my notes: things that are important to the class, and things that I will need to read over and over again in order to memorize. By the time you finish the chapter, not only will you have a fair outline of what's inside it, but the outline will be in your words, not theirs, making it easier to understand and memorize. Just make sure you wrote things down correctly before studying them too hard.

As for the style of the notes themselves, it really comes down to what works for you personally. I started out taking notes one way, then switched to a second way a month later, then switched to my current way the month after that. I use one giant binder divided up into five sections for my five classes. The dividers have pockets for me to cram papers into, and the fact that all my classes are in one binder makes it easy for me to know which binder to grab when I'm in a hurry. But that might not work for you.

There are a few different ways to take notes, I encourage you to go through them and see what works for you. I'll go through my personal study method, and then we'll tackle one that's a bit more popular and structured. I've been taking notes like this for about a year now, and it's worked fairly well for me.

It starts with a blank piece of paper. I don't type my notes on a computer, and I don't think you should either. Physically writing things down helps lock them into your memory, and it's also just plain easier to do. You don't have to wait for your piece of paper to boot up, your pencil doesn't freeze every once in a while, and you can afford to be more creative with your note-taking with a pencil and paper.

For example, the teacher clicks over to a slide with a diagram on it, and begins explaining it. If you have a pencil and paper you just draw a quick sketch of the diagram and go back to listening to the prof, maybe jot some clarifying points below your drawing. If you were on a computer you'd probably still be trying to draw that darn diagram using your note-taking software.

I also use a pencil, not a pen. I'm not perfect, I sometimes make mistakes. Erasers are your friend at that point. I used to use a standard wood pencil, but that stopped after the time I had to write a three hour English Literature exam with a pencil duller than a tube of Chapstick. Mechanical pencils are cheap, work well, and never get dull.

Put the chapter at the top, maybe the date and time on the right if you want, and get started taking notes. Some profs will either consciously or subconsciously drop hints that help you take notes, whether it's saying things like "this chapter focuses on four main theories...", or "there are three main key points to remember about this event...", or "you should write this down, as it will almost certainly be on the exam..." Not kidding on that last one, I've had more than a few profs stop in the middle of class and insist that everyone write a certain piece of information down.

Group your notes into headings, that you can underline. For example, if you were in Philosophy class, and the teacher said you were going to cover the works of Socrates, Plato, and Aristotle today, starting with Socrates. Your notes might look like:

Three Philosophers
- Socrates
- Plato
- Aristotle

Socrates
- "I know that I do not know"
  o Foundation of philosophy
  o In order to learn something, one must admit they do not know it already

And you would go on writing points and subpoints about Socrates until the prof switched to talking about Plato. By the end of the lecture you'd have a pretty good outline of what they had said, that you could go back to and review later. The problem is that not all lectures are organized like that one.

Sometimes the prof will jump around to different topics, or just start talking without mentioning any sort of structure. What do you do then? Well, you do your best, and then you go back after class and reshape your notes into a form that makes sense. Or you go up to someone else in the class and ask them if they understood a word of what the prof said either. Hey, you've made another new friend!

When it comes time to review for tests or exams, I practice what I like to call the "reductio ad absurdum" style of studying. Literally it means "reduction to the absurd", and that's fairly close to what it means for my note-taking style. To study, I'll take my notes, and read over them word by word. Then I'll write down everything I haven't memorized already, along with any dates and/or numbers that I need to memorize.

Then I'll read that summarized version of my notes a few times, until I'm fairly certain I know it, and then I'll construct a summarized version of the summarized version, and read that. This process goes on and on until I'm left with a page or two of highly-summarized notes that nobody but me could ever understand.

I review my page or two of gibberish every couple of hours until the test or exam hits, and I usually do fairly well. But the important part is that I don't just read it over and over and over again, that's no way to learn anything. To prove to myself I've memorized the notes, I do one of two things: either cover up all the sub-bullet points under a heading and try to recite them from memory, or cover up the heading and try to remember what it is from reading the sub-bullet points.

So that's my method of taking notes: I like it, and I especially like my studying method, as it's much more time-effective to only study what you don't know, rather than studying everything at once. It's pretty structured, but there's another method that is downright regimental, and it might be just what you're looking for. It's called the Cornell Method of note taking.

First off, you need a special piece of paper. Well, not so much that the paper itself is special, but what you put on it. You need to divide it up into three main segments:

1. The note-taking section
   a. This will be the largest section of the page, taking up about 2/3 of the width and 3/4 of the length.
   b. This is where you write the main notes that you're taking—dates, names, numbers, formulas, etc.
2. The keyword column
   a. This is where you write key phrases to help you remember what you wrote in the note-taking section.
3. The summary section
   a. Comprising about two inches or five-six lines at the bottom of the page, this section acts as a way to stimulate the memory by summarizing the content of the page into a few lines.

The whole thing seems a bit complex for me to deal with, but if you're the kind of person who prefers to have things extraordinarily organized, or if you are trying to become that kind of person, this might be right up your alley. In the end, both methods highlight the five Rs of studying:

1. **Record** – like I said before, if you don't write it down, you're going to forget it.
2. **Reduce** – your brain only has so much space in it. Fit more in by using summarized versions.
3. **Recite** – reading your notes repeatedly doesn't embed them in your brain like reciting them from memory does.
4. **Reflect** – schedule in some time to think about the material. Not everything is memorizing, take time to get the big picture.
5. **Review** – do it quickly and frequently, rather than in a few mega-sized chunks.

And there you go, you've taken your first class' worth of notes. Now you should introduce yourself to the professor. If you're in a class of 250 students, your prof will likely never know your name. Can you blame them? I sometimes have trouble remembering to pick up milk from the grocery store, let alone memorize 250 names every four months. That's why it's important for you to make the first effort, and let the prof know that you're there, and looking forward to spending two hours every week listening to them talk. They're people too, and who doesn't like it when someone compliments them?

<u>Review</u>

So, as you should be doing with your notes after class, let's review. You started off way back in high school, a blob of clay waiting to be sculpted. Then you sat down and did some thinking, and came up with what you wanted to do with your life. From that, you chose a university that would help you reach those goals.

You successfully moved in to university, started to find your way around the campus and the city, bought your textbooks, and went to your first class (you did go, right?). Once there, you learned how to take detailed notes that make sense to you, and how to organize your workload so you don't get slammed right before exams. It's been quite the week, hasn't it?

Chapter Three

Midterm Madness

So now we're going to skip ahead a bit. Imagine the next month and a half flying by—you keep reading the textbooks, doing the assignments, going to the classes, taking the notes, and reviewing them. On the other side, you're joining clubs and societies and such, or just making random friends. You go to a football game or a hockey game to cheer on the school team, and you're starting to settle into a routine.

Ah, routine. That's the important thing to have in university sometimes, it keeps you on track in the early morning so you don't forget to do something that's important, like put on pants. Not that that's ever happened to me. But like most people, I tend to be a bit groggy when I wake up, so it's good to have some sort of simple order to my day to keep things rolling along while my brain is still booting up. It usually goes something like this:

- Get up, shower, get dressed, etc.
- Grab backpack
  o Load up your binder, textbooks, etc. the night before
- Go to cafeteria, get breakfast
  o We'll go into nutrition later, but for now I'll just say: eat breakfast
- Eat cereal on way to class
- Actually wake up

Your routine doesn't have to be the same as mine, just try and have some sort of schedule to get you through your mornings prepared for the day.

But now it's time for that lovely routine to fall to pieces. Yes, it's midterm season. Here's another big difference between high school and university: in high school, you had multiple assignments and tests and quizzes, that all factored equally into your mark. You would get a mark for your first term, a mark for your second term, and an exam mark, and together they would be your grade. Things change a little bit in university.

For example, you have much less work that gets graded, but it's worth much much more. For example, in one of my first year courses my marks broke down like this:

- Term paper – 20%
- Midterm – 20%
- Exam – 60%

And that was it. The entirety of four months of my life essentially came down to three days. You can bet I worked my hardest to be on top of my game for those three days. How did I do it? That's what this next part of the book is all about.

The tricky part about midterms is that unlike exams, they tend to happen while classes and other things are still going on. So time management becomes even more essential. Ashamedly, I've had more than one occasion when I realized "Ah! I have a midterm next class!" It's very easy to let them slip into the flow with the rest of your classes, but you shouldn't do that.

An easy way to prevent this is with the day planner or calendar that you're keeping. I usually write down something like "Physics midterm in one month", "Physics midterm in one week", and other reminders to give you plenty of time to study up. And study you shall. But where?

Finding a good place to study on campus is like finding a great new band—you want to tell everyone about it, but you also don't want it to become too popular, because that would ruin it. Where you study on campus will depend on what your campus offers, but here are a few classic examples:

Library – This is the classic studying place. It's quiet, and there are plenty of people around you who are studying, to make you feel bad if you start to slack off. And if you feel like totally shutting yourself off from the world, there are usually things called study carrels that involve a chair, a desk, and near total sensory deprivation.

I studied in the library for the first couple of months during university, but it wasn't for me. I get distracted easily, and the lack of distractions in the library was, well, distracting. Your mileage may vary, though. All I know is that whenever I walk by the library at school now, I always see people with their noses in books and it makes me feel guilty for not studying.

Your room – This can be a very good idea, or a very bad idea, depending on where you live and when you do it. It's a good idea because it's close: you can just pick up a textbook, sit on your bed, and start reading.

I've done that quite a few times. Did it this morning, in fact. But sitting in your room means that other things are close by, like your television or your computer. So it can be tricky.

As to time, consider when you're doing your studying. If you're up all night writing a paper (which you shouldn't be, but that's for later), then it should likely be fairly quiet. However, if you expect your floor to be quiet at 9 PM on a Saturday night, you might want to remember what planet you're living on.

Computer lab – This is an interesting hybrid of the two, and it's the one that I most frequently do. Unsurprisingly, a lot of the work you're going to be required to do involves the use of a computer, so you may as well get used to your campus' computer labs. Oftentimes the chairs there are more comfy than the ones in your room, and they might even have sound-reducing panels on the walls.

For the best possible study experience, I essentially camp out in a computer lab for the day. I arrive early in the morning with my textbooks, and take a seat. I read a chapter or two, review my notes, then take a study break on the computer. Then I read a chapter or two more, review my notes, and have lunch.

The good part about having a readily available computer is that you can instantaneously look up any facts you don't know. Also, since you're not using your own computer, you don't have access to your personal bookmarks, and you're not automatically logged into your favourite sites. For me, this small inconvenience makes me much more productive.

Laundry room – Our world is becoming busier and busier every day. Things are swirling along at an ever greater pace, and time to just kick back and do nothing is coming at an increasingly higher premium. That's where the laundry room kicks in. What makes this study spot hot is that you're basically stuck here for the duration of your clothes being washed, and then dried.

Of course, you could always leave, but then you run the risk of coming back to a heap of sopping wet laundry on the floor with your name on it. Psych majors can tell you that it's easier for people to do something bad if the people they harm aren't physically present at the time. What that means is that you leaving your laundry alone makes it a lot easier for someone to dump your stuff and take your machine.

So what do you do? Well, I brought textbooks. Sitting amid the hum of the washers and driers provides a calming white noise that you may find promotes concentration. Or it might annoy the heck out of you, in which case you could bring music or something. The point is, waiting for your laundry to be done is one of the few times that nobody expects you to be running a hundred miles an hour around campus trying to get everything done. Accept that, and relax.

Cafeteria – This is another one whose success will largely depend on when you try it. It has tables, chairs, and readily available food, which makes it a good place to hunker down for an extended study session, but you'll probably find your greatest success when it isn't lunchtime or suppertime.

I ended up writing the final copy of my Hamachi report in a computer lab, but I sketched out 95% of the outline while sitting off in a corner of the cafeteria at Saint Mary's. It was quiet, private, and I had plenty of space to work in. It worked out quite well.

Empty classroom – This one works especially well around exam time, when classes are out, but it's a bit of a roll of the dice. You basically go around campus, try to find a classroom that's open, and then study there. If you find one, you're almost guaranteed to be the only person who's there, and every classroom usually has at least one computer. It's an excellent spot if you can find it.

Off-campus – Who says you have to study at school? Find a quiet place in a park, go to a local coffee shop, find a table at your nearest public library, or go to another university's library. Who knows, maybe you'll be able to trick your brain into forgetting that you're studying.

Those are all great places to study, but now we'll focus on what to actually do once you're there. To my mind, this should happen in two parts:

1) Information Gathering

This can (and should) happen while class is still in session. This is the part where you go through your old notes and summarize them into easily digestible study bites. You should also see if your prof has put any of the presentations they used up online. Tip: Check your textbook manufacturer's website, sometimes profs just use the slides that come with the book.

You should also look for any old tests that may be lying around. Ask profs, TAs, your friends who've already taken the course, and check online. Collect your old assignments, and check with your prof to see if they have any exam study materials like practice midterms or question banks or things like that. Compose a list of all the study resources that you have for a certain class. It might look something like this:

- English – re-read old stories, review essays
- Math – re-read textbook chapters, review presentations and notes, do practice midterm
- Science – re-read textbook chapters, review lab notes, do online test simulation

2) Information Reviewing

Now that you know how much you have to study, you can begin budgeting time. This figure's a bit rounded, and varies from book to book, but I find that it usually takes me an hour to really read and understand a textbook chapter. Over time, you'll find out how long it takes you to study, and you can adjust your time spent accordingly.

Speaking of adjusting time, you may find that you don't need to spend as much time on one course as you do on another. This is perfectly normal, and it can help you study more efficiently. I mean really, why spend time studying something you already know when you could use that time to study something you don't? This ties into the time management skills that are so crucial to success in university.

Another tip—when you study, actually study. Turn off your phone, lock your door, and put yourself into it. Conversely, it's also important to set time limits. It could be as simple as "today I am going to study chapter one, and tomorrow I am going to study chapter two". Do what you said you would do, and then enjoy your free time!

Decompressing and de-stressing is an essential part of any study period at university. As much as you might want to, you really can't study for more than a few hours before your attention starts to drift. Similarly, it's always nice to set goals for yourself, and reward yourself for achieving those goals.

Back in my first year, I wrote four exams in five days. I promised myself that I would study hard for the four days I had exams, but that on the day I had no exams, I would relax and enjoy myself. So I worked hard for two days, spent a day just walking around downtown with an ice cream cone, and then spent two more days working hard. The break helped me stay focused, and also stay sane.

Something else you should consider is that you can't predict life. It could be that you'll get sick next week, or your buddy will win tickets to a show, or something else unpredictable. Build buffer time into your schedule, so that you don't miss out on the fun times life can just drop into your lap suddenly.

In the days leading up to the midterm, you'll probably feel nervous. This is normal—if you didn't feel nervous, it would either be a sign that you don't really care how you do on the test, or a sign that you're secretly a robot. Neither one is really desirable. All you can do is keep studying in short, frequent bursts, and keep doing things to reassure yourself that you know the material.

The night before the midterm, don't stay up all night. Seriously, this isn't rocket science, have you ever heard anyone say cramming is a good idea? Cramming will help you pass the exam, but I would hope that your target mark for these tests a little bit higher than 51. Some studies have shown that reviewing your notes right before bed can help lock them in, so I usually try to do one final giant all-encompassing review right before my head hits the pillow. Hey, if you're studying something boring, it might even help you sleep.

You should sleep six to eight hours, have some breakfast, and just generally go about your day like you normally would. Make yourself a one-page summary of anything you really need to memorize, and review it right before you go into the test. Formulas, mnemonic devices, cram them all into your brain and spill them back out as soon as you get your paper. Hey, it's legal, you didn't bring anything into the room except for your short-term memory.

The best thing about midterms is that they eventually end. Yes, one day you'll be sitting in class, and you'll realize that you're done, and that you don't have any more midterms. And it will be a glorious feeling. Time to celebrate! How? By going back home. This may or may not be a celebration, depending on how much you like your particular family. I like mine, so I was fairly happy to be going back.

Yes, Thanksgiving is the turning point for many students—you've made it far enough that you're pretty sure you won't die at university, maybe you have some marks back that either reinforce your positive study skills or give you a kick in the rear to improve them, and you get to see all your high school friends again. Again, this may or may not be a good thing, depending on your particular high school experience.

It might also be the first time you've seen your parents in person since you left in September. For many people it's the longest they've spent away from home in their entire life. It can be an emotional time, that's for sure. It's important that things go both ways—your parents should recognize that you may have changed since you left, but you should probably still ease them into it.

And that's how the weekend should generally roll along—you're different now, but you should give everyone some time to catch up to you. Consider it a transition time, give people a chance to get used to the new you. Apart from that, enjoy the turkey (unless you've turned vegetarian), pumpkin pie (unless you've started a crash diet), and relax on the couch with your family (unless your philosophy class has taught you to believe that couches are evil). But even if that last one is true, you can still stand beside the couch and chat.

Speaking of important relationships, you're probably about to have one end: your high school girlfriend or boyfriend. I'm sorry, but it's a cold statistical fact—a study published in the Journal of Personality and Social Psychology showed that 74% of undergrads broke off their high school romances by the end of first year, in something called "The Turkey Dump".

Before we go any further, it's worth pointing out that if you do get dumped, it's not because you are a "turkey", the phenomenon just gets its name from Thanksgiving. Still, they could have picked a less cruelly ironic time of year to do it, couldn't they? Hey, if it makes you feel any better, having it all happen at once means that when you get back, the guy or girl you've secretly had your eye on might also be newly single.

After your parents load you down with two metric tons of Thanksgiving leftovers "in case you get hungry" (believe me, this will happen, leave room in your suitcase), you'll be back on university campus with everyone else. A few classes later, and October is over. Halloween time! Yes, for all of you who haven't dressed up in years, it makes a surprising and inexplicable comeback in university.

It seems to me that Halloween starts off excellent, then becomes less and less cool as you go through the grades, and then becomes massively cool again in first year university. I don't know why it happens, but if anyone out there makes it their thesis, send me a copy.

Summary

We started off this chapter espousing the value of a routine. And then I immediately went and dove into the time of year where your routine is going to be beaten to pieces—midterm season. But it's an important time of year, a time where your mark is largely determined, so it's important to do well during it.

You learned how to study your notes, where to study your notes, when to study your notes, and what to do once midterms are finally over and done with. You may or may not have survived the turkey dump, and celebrated the chance to be whatever you want to be on Halloween night. You're two months into university life, and things are probably turning around for you by this point.

So congratulations! Now let's do more work! Unfortunately, I'm not kidding. The next chapter involves how to deal with that thing that's been hanging around in the back of your mind since the first day of class—your term paper. It's November, and it's probably due soon, so we may as well get started.

Chapter Four

Papers A'Plenty

I f you look back to that marking scheme in the last chapter, you'll see that there were three major marks in your term—midterm, paper, and exam. We're moving through those as they happen, and right now it's time to learn how to write a completely excellent paper.

It breaks down into three main segments:
1. The Research
2. The Writing
3. The Editing

First off, the research. As I've mentioned before, I was a touch of a loner back in high school. I mostly kept to myself, read my books, and had few friends. Ironically, this made me extremely good at researching arcane facts and information. I then grew up into the outgoing fun-loving person that I am today, and can now share the best of both worlds with you.

First tip—do the research. This one's pretty important, I'm not going to lie. If you don't do any research, then your research will probably be lacking. Hey, I don't make the logic rules, I just logic enforce them. What I'm saying is that if you try and write a paper on Elizabethan history off the top of your head, how do I put this gently… your paper might not be as good as it could be..

It's not your fault, most people just don't have a head for remembering all the kings of England in chronological order. If you do, feel free to skip this section, I won't mind. But for the rest of us we might need a bit of a refresher. Research is one of those things that you get better at it the more you do it, and to be honest, it can be a lot of fun learning new things!

Now I am about to say something that you are not allowed to tell your profs I told you: Wikipedia is actually pretty good. Not that you should use it as your only research tool (and you certainly shouldn't just copy and paste the article as your paper—you laugh, but people do it), but if you're just getting started on a topic, and you're not sure where to start, you could certainly do a lot worse than to load up the Wikipedia page on the topic and give yourself a primer.

In fact, most good Wikipedia articles include a consolidation of links to reputable sources at the bottom of the page, which can save you time and effort tracking them down. Read through those pages, and get a sense of your topic, and what it's all about—what are the main points? Are there any contentious issues debated within the community? Building a gradual and general understanding of your subject matter, rather than just learning individual non-connected facts, will help you later on.

If you're reading this in a library, take a look at a medical textbook. Humans have skeletons for support, without them we'd collapse into a pile of goo on the floor. Do you want your paper to be a pile of goo on the floor? No? Then consider building it a skeleton. Except this skeleton is not made out of bone, but words.

I find the easiest way to do this is to keep a simple Notepad document open while I do my research. Then, when I find something worth keeping, I can write it into my outline. If I come up with the perfect way to say something, I'll write it down then before I forget. After a few days of this, it can stretch to a few pages long.

It usually looks like this: I'll have the three main topics I want to cover in bullet points at the top of the document, followed by the opening paragraph, written in its entirety. Then I'll have the three main topics, and sub-bullets detailing what I want to talk about. If I'm feeling ambitious I might try and pre-write the transition sentences. And then I'll have the fully-written concluding paragraph at the bottom.

As I said before, your outline doesn't have to be fancy. I use Notepad, for crying out loud. At Razorwire I do a lot of writing, and due to my ridiculously high standards for myself it needs to be amazing. So when I get a great idea for something to write, I'll start writing down an outline wherever I can. It'll normally go something like this:

- Idea!
    - o What it is
    - o Why it's awesome
    - o More details

When I came up with the idea for this book, I was riding a bus. I wrote in the margins of the book I was reading at the time:

- Write a book
  - University guide
    - For students, written by a student!
    - Have better knowledge than other authors
  - Possible topics
    - Study skills
    - How to write a good paper
    - How to stay healthy
  - To do: research how to get a book published

That's just an excerpt, it went on like that for a while. Later, when I was writing my book proposal, I expanded it to fill an entire sheet of paper, and went into more detail about what I would cover, and how I would cover it. I'm currently referring to that outline right now as I write the book, it keeps me on track and focused.

Now that you have an excellent outline, we'll move on to the part where you actually write the paper. As I'm sure you learned in high school, any decent paper has a fairly rigid structure:

- Introduction
  - Start with an attention grabbing headline.
    - "Children are raised not by their parents, but by their siblings. On average, you spend more time with your brother or sister than with both parents. Shakespeare was a master of exploring this fact."
    - And he did. History can be fun!
  - Then you go into the part where you describe what the paper is about.
    - "This paper will examine the role of sibling rivalry in Shakespeare's plays."
  - Talk about what you're going to talk about.
    - "It will examine three main examples…"
  - Transition into your first topic.
    - "The first rivalry to be examined is from King Lear…"
  - Write about it.
    - End with a transition to your second topic
  - Second topic.
    - Transition to third topic
  - Write it.

- Transition to closing
o Close memorably. A good ending is just as important as a good beginning.
  - "From these examples, we see that rivalry among siblings does not lead to a stable political system."

It's so easy to follow, it's a wonder why more people don't use it. Simply pop open your favourite word processor and start typing. Yes, just start typing. The trickiest part about an essay is getting away from that blank white page with a blinking cursor, so that's when it's great to already have your first paragraph written. Paste it in, and you're on your way! Start writing your second paragraph.

So you go through your first point, your second, third, and so on, finish it up with a strong conclusion, and you have a masterpiece of academia. Now save one copy in one place, back a second copy up somewhere else (do it), then go play Frisbee or watch TV or have dinner with a friend. Just get your mind off of the paper-writing track for the rest of the day.

The next morning, when you wake up, read your paper again. Again with the harsh truth, but it probably won't be as good as you remember. But lucky you, you have a chance to fix it up now. This is where the editing comes in. You've already made your words sing, now it's time to apply the AutoTune and make it sound absolutely perfect. However, just like music, too much AutoTune can make it sound phony and artificial, so make sure to retain your original intent with the writing.

If you know someone who's writing a paper for the same class, offer to swap drafts and edit each other's work. It's fun, you'll meet new people, and your finished product will be better for it. Do not believe Microsoft Word's grammar checker, its accuracy ranges from "picks the worse of two options" to "is actually flagrantly wrong".

Two quick grammar tips that will raise your perceived IQ by a few points: for a contraction, use it's. For a possessive, use its. I once had a prof who put in his syllabus, "If you hand me a paper that misuses it's and its, I will personally change as many of your current and past grades as possible."

If you're not sure which one to use, think of what the sentence would like if you put "it is" in place of the word, i.e. "the cat licked it is paws". See? Its simple. Whoops. I mean it's simple.

Also, the difference between who and whom is largely determined who's doing what. For example, the sentence "who saw you?" features you as the subject and who as the object. But "whom did you see?" has the roles switched, where you are the object and whom is the subject. It's tricky, but this is the one that if you can pull it off you'll look spectacularly intelligent.

What I've found to be a good way of proofreading papers is this: print if off, go for a walk, read it out loud. Trust me, if your writing doesn't flow, you'll find it in short haste. Plus you can practice your public speaking skills, which are important since you'll likely be giving quite a few presentations during your time at university.

Here's a sample itinerary you can follow to make sure you're on track for an A+ paper.

T-minus two months
- Begin brainstorming paper ideas
- Begin doing preliminary research

T-minus one month
- Finish gathering information
- Begin to create outline of essay

T-minus two weeks
- Write complete rough draft of paper
  o Doesn't have to be all at once, just have it done
- Set paper aside for a day or two, then review
  o Make obvious changes, then set aside again

T-minus one week
- Compose final draft
  o Set aside one more time, then compose final final draft
- Pass in paper

T-minus one day
- Resist mocking those who didn't follow this schedule
- Sleep well. You've earned it!

Summary

As I said before, paper writing is essentially a simple task: you take a subject, you research it, come up with an outline of what you want to say, make that outline into a full paper, edit the full paper, edit it again a few more times, edit it one more time, and then pass it in. The next chapter is where the tricky part comes in.

Your first semester is coming to an end, it's almost December, and in December comes the most wonderful time of the year. Yes, exam season is almost here. Read on to find out how to deal with it!

Chapter Five

Exams. Excited?

Exams are the most important part of your semester. Everything you've learned up until this point will be put to the test. How? By locking you in a gymnasium for three hours with a piece of paper and a pencil. In this chapter, we'll go over how to survive exam season, as well as what's to come after it's all finished.

As a lot of these chapters do, we'll start back at the beginning of the year. Most people believe that you should start studying for exams when exams themselves start, and this is largely true, but there's a bit of prep work you can do beforehand that will make things easier for you.

For example, you can approach them largely the same way you approached the midterm: start gathering your information early. You can do this by collecting up your notes from the entire semester, and summarizing them into what I call "study packs". These would be multi-page documents that highlight, line by line, everything you've covered over the past four months.

If that sounds like a lot of work, that's because it is. But hey, nobody said exams were going to be easy. Approach study packs with this notion: If you were asked to summarize all of your notes into one document, what would you write? Let's say the first thing you learned in Statistics class was how to calculate mean, median, and mode. You would start by writing down, in detail, how to do that.

Then you'd move on to the second topic you covered, and the third, and before you know it, all of your notes are consolidated into one place, written in words you can understand, in an order that makes sense. Not only does this make it extremely easy to study, but there are two advantages you can gain simply by creating a study pack.

First, even if your study pack is just a carbon copy of your original notes, rewriting them puts them fresh in your brain again. But it's more than likely that when you review your old notes, you'll think of new ways you could have written the same thing. Without the time pressure of a professor moving on with their lecture, you may find that you can rewrite your notes in a more understandable fashion (or at least a more legible fashion).

By going through this rewriting process and really thinking about what you're writing about, you'll find the best and simplest way of explaining how to do a problem. As a nice bonus, the simplest way of doing something is usually also the quickest, easiest to memorize, and hardest to screw up.

More steps means more to memorize, and more places to make a mistake. When I wrote my Statistics study pack I was able to reduce my process for calculating standard deviation from six steps to two. Which one do you think would be easier to recall on an exam?

As I said before, summarizing four months of notes into ten to twenty pages will take a while. But it's one of the most helpful things you can do to help yourself prepare for the exam. Instead of having to rummage through all of your notes, which may have been taken in different styles, different levels of detail, even your handwriting can vary from class to class, you'll have a single authoritative source that all knowledge flows from. Pair that with your textbook, add a few practice exams if your prof provides them, and you have an unbeatable study pack. Now it's time to use it.

Study groups can be helpful. Note that I said can be helpful. If you do it wrong, you'll end up worse off than before. Make sure that the people you study with are as dedicated as you are (or more so). Otherwise you'll just end up goofing off, which is a fun time, but won't help you solve a math problem. But on the positive side, helping other students can reinforce your own understanding of the material—if you can't teach it, or even describe it, how well do you really know it?

Go to your final classes. Go to all of your classes, obviously, but some people seem to think they can drop off the last few and use them to study (or not study). Trust me, spending an hour with your prof will be more productive than spending an hour in the library. And it'll certainly help you more than an hour in your bed.

As an incentive, most profs will usually take questions and describe a general outline of the exam for the people who attend. How much detail they reveal varies from prof to prof—some will just tell you what format it is, some will tell you certain chapters/topics to focus on, I've even had a couple cases where the prof said "Here's a question that's going to be on the exam. Study it." It really depends.

And then the class time ends, and you're left with nothing but the notes you took, and the attention you paid while you were in class. Exam season is here, and you'd better be ready for it.

How you study, when you study, what you study. All of these things will be largely determined by your exam schedule. It usually starts in early December or mid-April, and you can have class at any time of day, on any day, in any frequency. Yes, Saturday morning exams are possible. Yes, they do coffee is necessary.

I've known people who had:
- five exams on the first five days of exam period
- five exams on the last five days of exam period
- five exams in three days
- five exams evenly spaced throughout the entire exam period (lucky)

My first exam schedule involved five exams in six days. It was tough, but I got through it. As I said before, everything essentially comes down to your exam schedule. So once your prof announces it or it's posted at the Registrar or put up online, copy down your exam schedule into your calendar, and start blocking off some study time.

At the very least, plan to dedicate the entire day prior to your exam to studying exclusively for that course. Shut out all other distractions and focus on that one thing for at least one day. If you feel it will be a more difficult course (Calculus, for example), then it may be necessary to extend this period backwards until you hit another exam. It's when your exams get tightly bunched that things get interesting.

When you have two exams on the same day, or on back to back days, it basically comes down to a sense of priorities. Which class do you need to study for more? If they're equal, then study for them equally. Also, unless they're back to back exams, you should have some time between them where you can study exclusively for your second exam.

Most exam scheduling software is designed to minimize students writing back to back exams, but it's software, it screws up sometimes. Contact your prof or your student union, they may be able to help you out. If your exams don't start until the middle of the exam period, don't go home and plan to come back for your exams, especially in the winter. The weather can be your worst enemy.

Instead, use this time to do a general overview of all your classes. This way, you don't have to study everything later on, you can just focus on the finer points and really polish your knowledge to a blinding shine. Take your study packs, and go over them in detail. Tackle one per day if you have the time, then kick back and relax when you're done—it's easy to burn yourself out studying too hard.

As your exams draw near, study a little bit more and a little bit more, then do the practice exams and study what you had the most trouble with, and then do a gigantic overview of everything about everything the day before the exam. The night before the exam, read over your study pack in detail to lock it in your memory while you sleep.

Then wake up, have a good breakfast, and depending on when your exam is, either study or write it. However, I wouldn't advise bringing materials with you to the exam room, save for a pencil, watch, and your student ID. Maybe a ruler and calculator if you foresee needing them.

Note about the student IDs: Bring them. Your university likes you quite a bit, thinks you're a good guy/girl, but it still doesn't trust you enough to not hire someone to write your exam for you. It's been burned before, so either go write the exam yourself (preferred) or actually put some effort into your fraud and whip up a good-quality fake student ID for the person writing the exam in your place.

Disclaimer: don't actually do that. It's not recommended, probably illegal, and presented here only for the purposes of humour. On the plus side, if the school catches you, you won't have to worry about writing exams there ever again. Not to mention that in the time it would take you to learn how to properly counterfeit and produce a student ID, you could probably read your textbook twice over.

Once it's actually exam time, or close to it, you need to stop learning and start organizing. If you've ever tried to organize a messy closet, you'll understand what I'm about to say. When most people try to organize a closet, they start out by taking everything out at once, putting it in labeled storage containers, and then putting the containers back in the closet.

This is essentially what you're doing with your studying—you're taking all your old handouts, notes, memories, and textbook readings out of your brain, organizing them into study packs, and then putting them back in. That way, when your brain wants to know where the Sociology notes are, it can easily find them.

However, at this point of your studying, you still have the boxes scrambled out on the floor as you frantically throw more and more information into them. Always remember to take time to put the boxes away again. Otherwise you'll be so frazzled by the time you get to the exam room you won't be able to remember where you put anything.

If you like baking analogies, here's one for you—when you're making bread, there's a point where you've added all the ingredients, and now you just have to wait for them to mix together and make the bread rise. If you skip this step, you'll ruin the bread. By letting it sit and rise, the end result is much more delicious.

Before you leave your room to go to the exam room, review your notes one final time. All of them. Read your entire study pack over one more time, then read the parts that just don't seem to be fitting in one more time again. Run over them in your head to jam them in your memory. Then put it away and leave.

Arrive thirty minutes early. This will allow you plenty of time to calm yourself down, think, and relax before you take the exam. If it helps, imagine little elves running around inside your brain, taking all the notes you've spent time placing in there and filing them away in their proper places. By the time you go in to write the exam, your brain should be perfectly organized, and everything will fall into place.

Read the entire exam, front to back, when you get it. There's an old urban legend of the professor who handed out his final exam with the following written on the back page:

"If you hand this back to me within 5 minutes I'll give you an A+ and you can leave."

Again, this has probably never really happened, but it's a funny story to keep in mind. Professors, especially the ones with tenure (aka "can't be fired"), have a tendency to do some odd things to shake up their students.

Also, you'll get to see if there are any questions that you predict will take a while to do, and finish them first. During one of my accounting midterms, I came within two minutes of running out of time because of a monster question that had been placed at the back of the paper. When exam time rolled around, the first thing I did was check at the back of my exam, and there it was—another enormous question that would have totally blown my timeline.

Conversely, you may choose to do all the easy questions first, and then move on to the hard ones. This is a popular strategy, but it's one I've never really been interested in—they say that it allows you to start your exam off on a positive note, but I prefer to ration my easy questions throughout the exam for a periodic confidence booster.

In exam writing, as in most things related to university, time management is key. If you spend all your time on only half of the exam, you'd better be right on every one of those questions. Alternatively, budget your time according to point values. In my first year, my final exam was a one hundred question multiple choice test, each question worth one mark. Therefore, I knew that each question was only worth spending one percent of my time on. I ended up finishing all of the hundred in eighteen minutes, but that's beside the point.

If you're unsure about a part on the exam, ask! They won't give you the answer, but if you're just looking for clarification, this can be very helpful. For example, if you're writing a math exam, and there are two ways to solve it, and you know both of them but you're unsure which way to use, that would be an acceptable clarification.

Which of the following statements are incorrect?

a. Statement 1

b. Statement 2

c. Statement 3

d. All of the above are correct

This is the structure of a multiple choice question from one of my exams. Which exam is immaterial. What's important is examining the logical structure inside. If I choose d, I am saying that at least one of a, b, or c are incorrect. If I choose a, b, or c as incorrect, I am implying that d is correct. But if d is correct, a, b, and c must also be correct. You can see the problem.

I called my prof over, and he drew a large X through it with his pen, then told me that since I obviously possessed the underlying logical analysis skills the question was trying to test, I didn't have to answer it, I would just get the marks. Score!

Other quick tips are: if the answer involves the words "always" or "never", you should be very sure of yourself before making that your final answer. In my experience, those are rarely the correct answer. However, sometimes you'll get a prof who likes to be unconventional, so be on your toes.

If the question has "all of the above" as a possible answer, there are two possible reasons: one, that the prof is trying to trick you, or two, that it's actually the right answer. The easiest way to find out is to use a little bit of logic: you don't need to prove that all four are true, you only need to prove that two are true. If there are two true answers to the question, then either the prof screwed up, or one of them actually isn't a true answer and you don't know it, or "all of the above" is the correct answer.

For true/false questions, use this logical test: for the question to be true, all parts of the question must be true. For the question to be false, only one part of the question must be false. If you can pick one untrue statement out of a paragraph, your answer must be "false". There's a story that says that decades ago, all swans were believed to be white. The reason? Nobody had ever seen a black swan, so they must not exist. The statement "all swans are white" was true.

However, one day explorers were trekking through the deep, dark forest, and came across one black swan. They took photos, confirmed it was indeed a swan, and presto! The statement "all swans are white" could no longer be said to be true, because even though 99.99% of them are, that's a long way from 100%. Remember this when you're analyzing your true/false questions.

I once had a professor that did one of the best things to prepare me for the exam that they could. They took an entire class, and said "Alright. So we've been here for four months. The exam is only three hours long. How much do you realistically think we can put on it?" And that put things into perspective for me—there's only so much they can test you on in three hours and still expect you to finish.

So in a perfect world, yes, you should know everything. But you probably won't. That's when you need to hope that the things you don't know, and the things that were deemed not important enough for the exam, are the same. Think about your prof—what did they spend the most time on? What would logically make sense for them to focus on for the exam?

Always check your work. Sometimes you'll find that your answers don't make any sense. For example, back in high school I wrote a standardized exam in Physics. The question dealt with planetary gravitation—we were given the mass of one planet, the amount of gravitational attraction between them, and were supposed to solve for the mass of the second planet.

I went through all my meticulous calculations, and came up with the figure that the second planet would have a diameter of 3.1 billion metres. You science majors will know that the diameter of our own Sun is about 1.4 billion metres. I thought "it's possible that this is just a very large and purely theoretical planet, but just in case, I should check my math." I did, and there was an error.

I once had a prof that said, "If you can do the problem, and not know for sure at the end whether or not your answer is right, you haven't learned anything at all." And they're essentially right—in real life, the point of doing rigorous math problems is not to prove that you can do them, but to obtain information to help you make decisions.

So if you don't know what your answer means, and don't know how to use it, why spend all the time acquiring it in the first place? Imagine you took a course that taught you how to save money. You save your money for five years, wanting to buy a Lexus. You then get to the car lot and tell the salesperson that you don't have a driver's licence. You certainly know how to save money, but the exercise was absolutely pointless and a waste of everyone's time.

Keep your notes organized, even after midterms. A lot of exams will only test you on the material covered after the midterm, and some will just heavily weight it towards post-midterm material. However, that doesn't mean you should throw out your earlier notes (as I have done on more than one occasion).

Retaining a full understanding of everything you've done so far is key to answering things like essay questions and other tests of actual knowledge rather than rote memorization. Below are some other tips for answering various types of questions:

Multiple Choice

Deceptively simple. That's how I'd describe multiple choice questions. People look at them and think "they're not as hard as normal questions. I mean, come on, they give you the freakin' answer!" And this is true. Sort of. The answer is there, that's true, but it's nestled amongst (usually) three other answers that, in the heat of exam stress, can really seem like they're also the right answer.

The simplest way to do better on multiple choice is the following strategy. Evidence suggests that one in three students can do better on multiple choice tests simply by following this one tip: Read the question, and cover the answers. Then come up with the answer in your head. Only then will you uncover the answers. If it's there, great! It's probably the right one.

Let's break it down analytical-style. For every ABCD multiple choice question, there are normally three types of answers—tricks, almost-rights, and the actual right answer. Take a look at this question, that will probably be on more than one of your exams if you're in business:

Which of the following people is responsible for the term "scientific management"?

a) Frederick Taylor
b) Abraham Maslow
c) Carl Sagan
d) Ronald McDonald

Picking the right one can be tricky. In this example, A is the right answer. However, B is the almost-right answer—Abraham Maslow is behind Maslow's Hierarchy of Needs, which will probably crop up somewhere else in the exam. As for the tricks? Carl Sagan is a popular scientific TV host. And if you think Ronald McDonald is the correct answer, how did you get accepted to university in the first place?

Open Book Exams
Be afraid. Be very afraid. Granted, that might be a little extreme, but these are some of the toughest exams you'll ever write. Most people look forward to these exams, until they realize the key element of open book exams: they expect a whole lot more from you. And can you blame them? You have the darn textbook sitting in front of you, why shouldn't you be perfect?

And therein lies the challenge—the profs are expecting you to be perfect, and you probably won't be. So how do you do well on an open book exam? Same as any exam—study. Know as much as you can without having to open the textbook, and use the textbook as a fact-checking source for dates and places and names.

If you need to read the textbook during your exam, you've left your studying until too late. Do that before your exam. But you can make it easier to find the information you want. Depending on how militant your prof is, you may be able to use sticky notes or bookmarks to allow easy access to the pages containing key information that you know you'll need to look up at least once during the exam.

Essay

Contrary to the name, these questions often don't expect you to write a full essay, it gets its name from two parts: one, that your answer is expected to be at least a little bit longer and more thought-out than a standard question, and two, that you're expected to have some sort of essay-style form to your answer.

This would be the simple structure we discussed in the previous chapter: start off with a quick summation of your answer, include some more details, then wrap everything up in a nice conclusion. These questions are usually worth multiple points, so pay close attention to that. I once had a prof who, without telling us, expected us to write one paragraph for every point the question was worth. I paid a heavy price for my conciseness on that exam.

For example, there could be a question like this:

Some people believe that Ronald McDonald is the origin of the phrase "scientific management". Argue in favour of this belief.

Like I said, this is not the right answer. But the trick to essay questions isn't always in facts and figures, but in a deep understanding of the concepts you've learned. For example, scientific management is a method of analyzing processes to make them more efficient. In your essay, you would argue that McDonald's has perfected the process of serving fast food (any person who's worked at McDonald's can tell you just how precise some of their regulations are).

You'd set up your essay with an introduction comparing the two, a few paragraphs going into more detail, and then wrap up by demonstrating their similarities. Full marks!

So now you've done your first exam. Congratulations! That wasn't so bad, now was it? If it was, how could you improve for next time? Think, ponder, consider, and then do it! If you're taking a normal schedule you'll have four more chances to get it right, and I'm fairly sure you will eventually.

For your second exam, and the ones that follow, it's pretty much the same structure:

- Start with general studying
- Focus in as the day approaches
- Study as hard as you can the day before
- Finish things up and polish your knowledge the day of

- Show up thirty minutes early
  o Organize your metaphorical closet or let your metaphorical bread rise
- Write the exam, know you did well, and enjoy!

Summary

As I've said before, exam times are weird times. They comprise the minority of your class time, but the majority of your mark. But by following the strategies I've outlined in this chapter, you can make the most of them. Plus, now that exams are over, do you know what time it is?

Winter Break! It truly is the most wonderful time of the year. You have no classes, so you can't possibly have anything to work on. It's a fantastically freeing feeling. However, keep in mind the same notes that I mentioned back during Thanksgiving—your family may not immediately accept that you are a different person now, so give them time to acclimate to the new you. Besides, taking part in a few old family traditions might still be fun.

Chapter Six

You're Baaack....

Happy New Year! How was your winter break? I hope you had some quality family time, and a chance to reflect on everything you've accomplished over the past semester. The winter break after my first semester was when I first wrote the Facebook note that became this book. Let's take a look at everything you've done so far, and all the things you've learned:

- How to choose a university
- How to choose a career
- How to move in to university and get settled
- How to save money on textbooks
- How to handle your first week
- How to keep organized, and take notes
- How to study for midterms
- How to write a great paper
- How to survive exam season

Now it's time to do it all over again! Huzzah! Yes, it's time for another semester at school. If you're taking mostly full-year courses this might be easier for you, but a lot of places have broken up their courses into two parts to make it easier for students to jumble their schedules as necessary. This means that you need to find new classrooms, take new notes, and try your best to improve over last semester.

And how do you improve? Well that basically comes down to you—how did your first semester go? Take some time for introspection, and determine what you need to work on—maybe you need to take more understandable notes, or spend more time reading your textbooks for detail rather than just skimming them. Maybe you need to go to class more than you did in the first semester. It's all up to you.

For myself, I usually use a three part process to evaluate how my year has gone, and I encourage everyone I know to do the same thing. It helps you summarize what you've been able to accomplish in the past year, and what you hope for in the next year. It breaks down into three parts: Social, Academic, and Personal.

Social

For some people, sociality comes as easily as breathing. For some people, it's a tireless struggle to fit in. I was in the second category, but I worked long and hard to make things easier for myself. Now, I feel completely at ease in a group of people, but still like to keep to myself at times.

So the test is essentially this: Did you meet new people? Forge new bonds with friends, and students? If not, why not? You'd be hard pressed to find a more sociable place in the world than a university campus. That doesn't mean it's always easy to find friends, it takes time to develop relationships and meet people.

But, if you're at the end of your first year and you haven't met even one person that you can remotely stand, I think that's something worth pondering on. Join a society, go to a sports game, ask to borrow a pencil from the person who sits next to you in class. Smile! Connect with the people in your life, and they will connect back to you.

However, it can take a long time. Sometimes opening yourself up to new people can feel like throwing yourself against a door: it hurts when it stays closed, but every once in a while the door will swing open. It won't open if you don't try, and blaming the door for not opening isn't going to help you out either. The only way in is to keep throwing yourself against that door and know that it will eventually open.

In the end, for all the talk about it, books written and seminars given, it's actually fairly easy to make friends. Say hi to all the people you meet, and introduce yourself to the ones that say hi back. Then you chat about your classes, and other things, you find out what they're interested in, and you find out if you like them. If you've gotten this far, they probably like you too, so presto! New friend.

Academic

This is the one that the majority of this book is dedicated to, because really, this is why you're here—to learn. If you were here to make new friends for four years, you could just hang out on campus all day and not have to pay tuition. Academia is what you're here for, and it should be your focus. Some people take this too far and refuse to do anything but study, and that's not optimal either.

All three parts of this system work in balance, but Academic should probably be your biggest chunk. Luckily, it's much easier to assess your academic skills than your social skills, the university even does it for you and posts the results online. All you need to do is take those numbers, and compare them against what you want to be achieving.

This will vary from person to person. Some people don't care about marks, as long as they're above an F. Some people break down in tears when they don't get an A. After talking to profs, I've found that the second category are not only more likely to complain about their marks, but are more annoying when they do so.

Some students have too much of their self-worth tied up in their GPA, and they feel that they have to get an A or their life is a failure. And that's a load of rubbish. Yes, good grades are important, especially if you're on scholarship, but you also have to consider what you've learned.

I'll use two courses as an example, with the names hidden to avoid hurting anyone's feelings. In Course X, I learned something every day, and expanded my horizons beyond where I knew they could be. In Course Y, I doodled during every class, and spent most of the time thinking about the concepts I'd learned in Course X instead. I received a B+ in Course X, and an A+ in Course Y.

And I will tell you, if I could only choose one, I'd choose to have a B+ average and love my classes over having an A+ average and a rotted brain. However, I luckily don't have to make this choice, as I also like keeping my scholarship, which requires an A- average. So I compromise by working my hardest in all my classes, not just the ones that interest me. In return, Saint Mary's gives me a considerable sum of money. I guess it works out for the best in the end.

So what I'm saying is this: work hard, get good grades, but always make sure to hold your performance against nobody's standards but your own and your university's. You're there to learn, and when that happens the grades follow naturally.

Personal

This one's usually the trickiest, and it's the one you should spend the most time pondering on—did you become a better person in the past year? There are a million different ways you could measure this, but you'll know the answer if you ask yourself. Maybe you became a better public speaker, or a better writer, or a better researcher, or just became more willing to smile and help people out. It's tricky to pin down when you improve as a person, but you can find it when you look for it. Sorry I can't write more on it, it just has to come from inside.

Summary

Have you ever tried writing the summary for a chapter that's already a summary? It's difficult. I guess I'll just say that I truly enjoyed writing this book, hopefully it helps you survive your university experience. Trust me, it's worth it.

The rest of this book is comprised of chapters that each focus on a specific skill, such as exercise, teamwork, or nutrition. And after that are a few appendices that I felt would improve the book's overall quality.

Chapter Seven

Exercise:
One Action, Many Results

What if I told you there was something that would not only make you look better, feel better, help you out in school, and make your thoughts clearer, but was also a lot of fun? The simple answer is exercise. Simply finding time for a little physical activity in your day will pay dividends in every other area of your life, guaranteed. It is, quite simply, one of the most important things you can do in your life. So how do you get started on it? That's the great part—you can start whenever you want. Heck, you could decide to put down this book and go for a walk right now.

However, I'd prefer it if you took this book with you on that walk, as I have a few more pages to go on how to get the most out of your exercise. My first tip is that most of the problems you're going to encounter are entirely mental. Granted, you will likely encounter physical problems, but they can be mostly overcome by a good stretching program and using a bit of common sense in your workouts.

The mental part is a bit trickier. Motivating yourself to exercise shouldn't be difficult, but for some reason it is. Go figure. In psychology and management classes you can study motivation until your brain falls out onto the floor, but for now the only thing is to learn how to deal with them. I'll start with the most common problem: persistence.

Here's John the university student. John wants to get in better shape, so he says "I'm going to work out every day!" And for a week or two, he does. But then something comes up, and he misses a day of exercise. He is seriously bummed out by this. "Now everything's ruined!" he says, and stops exercising. That doesn't work.

Here's Jake the university student. He also wants to get in better shape, so he also says "I'm going to work out every day!" And for a week or two, he does. But then something comes up, and he misses a day of exercise. He says, "Oh well, that's life." and gets back to his regular schedule the very next day. Who do you think actually loses weight: John or Jake? Persistence is key, missing one day doesn't mean you have to quit.

Heck, missing a week doesn't mean you have to quit. Do what you need to do, and get back to the gym as soon as possible. That's all.

The second problem is not knowing what you're doing. The old saying goes that "practice makes perfect". But if your practice is flawed, you're just reinforcing negative habits. So really, "perfect practice makes perfect". Perfect may be a bit of an exaggeration, but hopefully you understand what I mean. If you are working out at a gym, then you likely have staff there that can help you out.

Check if they have a free "New Member Orientation" session that you can attend, where they take you around and show you the different machines. In fact, many places are required by law to make sure you understand how to use the machines safely before they're allowed to let you work out on them. Use this to make your workouts as safe and practical as possible.

As with anything, having a plan is essential to success. Have an exercise routine that you can run through consistently, one that's comprehensive and effective in improving your body, and something you can stick to over the long haul. The two main topics in exercise this book will cover are the FIT principle, and the two major types of exercise.

First is the FIT principle. It's an acronym that stands for Frequency, Intensity, Time. These three things make up how effective your workout can be, and they also form the basis of how you can modify your workout if need be.

Frequency is how often you work out. I work out before my classes Monday to Thursday, four days a week. If I wanted to increase that, I could start getting up early on days when I don't have class (not bloody likely) to work out. It's fairly simple: working out more gives better results.

Intensity is how hard I work out. Say I go on a treadmill and do a brisk walk at level 3.5. I could mix things up by throwing in the occasional jog at level 6.0 if I wanted. This would make for a more intense workout. And finally, Time. I work out for seventy-five minutes, because that's the length of my break between classes, making it easy to fit exercise into my schedule. If I wanted to work out for ninety minutes, that would give better results.

As you can see, it's a fairly simple concept to grasp. If you ever feel like your current workout isn't challenging you enough, just think, "What can I change? Will I work out more often, more intensely, or longer?" I wouldn't advise changing too quickly—if you go from working out twice a week to four times a week, it's probably not the best time to also ratchet up the intensity or duration of your workout.

Moving on, there are basically two types of exercise: cardiovascular, and weight training. Cardio consists of things like running on a treadmill, pedaling on a stationary bike, or stepping on a stair machine. They get your heart rate up, get your blood pumping, and increase your breathing rate. Consistent cardio exercise will strengthen your heart and lungs, making it easier to run for the bus when you really need to.

You're laughing, but that was the first benefit I noticed when I first started working out. I would always be running for the bus, and over time I noticed it got easier and easier as I became more cardiovascularly fit. The sad part about this is that it's not very flashy. If you're looking for something to show off, a great cardiovascular system is a bit tricky to show people. But it is important.

If you just want to look great at the pool, then strength training is for you. This is the other major stuff people think of when they think of the gym: bicep curls, bench presses, and other things. You may feel initially uneasy about weight training, as it's the section of the gym that tends to attract people who look like they set up a cot in the corner and sleep in the gym.

But in reality, I've found that if you leave them alone, they'll leave you alone. Everyone is there for one purpose: to get physically fit. And hey, they obviously know how to use the machines, and probably wouldn't mind showing you a few tips. Don't fear the weight room, is what I'm saying.

I won't provide any specifics for how you should exercise, or how much, or anything of that nature, that's for you and your gym staff to determine based your unique situation. However, there are certain cautions you should take when working out, no matter who you are. This leads into the third problem I see with people new to exercise.

The third problem is doing it wrong, or too much. As a rule, if you're too stiff and/or sore to do the exercise, maybe you should reconsider doing the exercise. I do a lot of pushups, but I can't do them every day because my body physically won't allow me to. I could certainly "push through the pain" and force myself to do more pushups, but that's for professional athletes who have coaches and physiotherapists dedicated to helping them heal. You don't have that. So stay reasonable.

Again, what you do have is the gym staff. They usually have at least some sort of training in this area, and can provide you with tips on how to maximize your workout. For instance, I work the muscles in my upper body on Monday and Wednesday, and the muscles in my lower body on Tuesday and Thursday. No days wasted, no extra chance of hurting myself. That's just my experience, your gym staff will have different tips for you.

But isn't exercising expensive? Gym memberships are costly, you have to buy specialized clothing, sports drinks, it all adds up. Or does it? I work out in an old pair of shorts and a t-shirt. My water bottle is filled with water, not HyperMegaPerfomanceExtreme Juice. Even my gym membership is included in my tuition, and yours might be too.

And if it isn't, you don't even really need the gym to work out. You can do pushups on the floor of your residence room, run up and down the stairs for cardio, and other creative ways of exercise. If that's too daunting, take the stairs instead of the elevator. If you live on the twentieth floor of your residence building, take ten floors of stairs and ten on the elevator. Chances for exercise are everywhere if you look for them.

Chapter Eight

Nutrition:
Fighting The Freshmen 15

We, as humans, are pretty simple creatures. We require few things to sustain our life—water, food, sleep, oxygen, that's about it. So why is it often so hard to meet these basic needs? That's what this section will be all about.

First, water. The basis of human life, water comprises the majority of your body. Blood is 95 percent water, and even bones are 22 percent water. Your body uses it to regulate your temperature, fuel your brain and organs, and generally keep you a happy student. Therefore, it's quite important that you keep your body well-hydrated. But how do you do that?

First off, you don't need to drink eight glasses of water a day. That's ridiculous. You can if you want, but it's certainly not necessary for your health. In fact, not all your water even needs to come from water. Fruits and vegetables have plenty of moisture in them, as do bread and meat. And although it's not the ideal source, coffee and/or alcohol do provide your body with fluid. You lose about a third of it due to alcohol and caffeine being diuretics (makes you have to urinate), but they'll work in a pinch.

In fact, some studies have even shown that your body builds a tolerance to caffeine, and lowers its diuretic effects. You may think that this means sports drinks are the key to good hydration, and they can certainly help. But they're expensive. If you take a glass of orange juice, and throw a pinch of salt in it, you've just created 95 percent of a sports drink for 5 percent of the cost.

The bottom line is this: everyone is different. Someone who is a varsity athlete might require a bit more water than someone who is a varsity mathlete. Instead of drinking an arbitrary amount of water every day, you should drink when you're thirsty, and not force water on yourself. Simple.

Now that we've covered drink, let's move on to food. Ah, glorious food. To some it's merely a source of fuel, to others it's a sensory experience. In my life, I switch between the two depending on how busy I am that day. I've run the gamut from spending hours preparing an elaborate feast to chowing down on an energy bar while I ran for the bus. But the fact remains: food is important. It breaks down into a few different categories, each providing something essential to your life: carbohydrates, fats, fiber, minerals, protein, vitamins, and water. Of these, they are either macronutrients (you need a lot of them) or micronutrients (you only need a little of them).

Carbohydrates, or "carbs", are the basis of human energy. They are found in things like bread, pasta, and sugar. Recently, the Atkins diet proclaimed to help people lose weight through a low-carbohydrate/high-protein diet. Note: any diet that says you can eat as much bacon as you want and still lose weight should really be a red flag.

The diet was largely successful due to the fact that it involved cutting out your body's main energy source, forcing it into a starvation state where it burned stored calories. But then the founder died, and rumours began to circulate. Officially, he fell and hit his head while shoveling snow. But nobody knows what caused him to fall in the first place. Could have been ice, but some say it was a heart attack.

If you're a Chemistry major, you already know what fat is—a long chain of carbon and hydrogen atoms bonded to a glycerol, forming a triester. But for most people it's something found in food, such as the cheeseburger you ate during your last night out downtown. And I know how satisfying that can be, but it's important to keep track of your fat intake. Otherwise you can put yourself at risk for heart disease, stroke, and a wide array of other problems.

Not all fats are bad. Here's where it gets complicated: you have saturated fats and unsaturated fats. Saturated fats have all their carbons bonded to their hydrogens, whereas unsaturated fats have fewer hydrogens than carbons. And depending on how big the difference is, they can be either monounsaturated or polyunsaturated. And then depending on which hydrogen is missing, they can be either Omega-3 or Omega-6 fatty acids. As previously mentioned, if you're not a Chemistry major you likely don't need to understand the past paragraph, so don't worry. Just know that unsaturated is best for you, especially monounsaturated, followed by saturated, and then we come to trans fats.

You should worry about trans fats. These are the weird kids in the fat family—trans fats don't usually occur in natural food, they have to be created in labs for purposes multiple and nefarious. Their differentiating feature is that they have trans-isomer bonds, which can only reliably be created under controlled conditions, through a process known as "hydrogenation".

Hydrogenation is where they force more hydrogen than is normally present or should naturally be there into a molecule, creating results that are good for the people making it (longer shelf life for the food) and bad for you (shorter shelf life for your body). The next segment is fiber, because it's really unpleasant when you don't get enough of it.

Fiber is essentially a different form of carbohydrates, in that it cannot be absorbed by the human body, but it performs several important functions while it is there. It's broken down into two different kinds: soluble fiber and insoluble fiber. I realize that this has been a fairly chem-heavy chapter so far, but bear with me when I say that soluble fiber is dissolvable in water, and insoluble fiber isn't.

Good places to get fiber are from vegetables, whole grains, and fruits such as plums, prunes, and figs. Perhaps your university dining hall offers a bran cereal you could try out every once in a while. Not only does fiber aid your digestion and help you absorb nutrients more completely, but there are studies showing that it can lower your risk of heart disease. And if you're diabetic, a healthy dose of fiber can reduce insulin spikes from the food you consume, which is nice.

If carbohydrates are the fuel of your body, then protein is the oil that keeps it running smoothly. Protein builds your muscles, your hair, your skin, and many of the other things about your body. But these proteins need to be replaced every once in a while when they die off or are damaged. Amino acids are the primary chemicals that make up proteins, so consuming sources of protein allows your body to break it down into individual amino acids, which can then be used to rebuild the proteins it currently requires.

It's kind of like building Lego—you need a certain set of bricks to build a house, so you disassemble the Lego car you built earlier and remake it in a new shape. The bricks are amino acids that you can put together in different arrangements to make different creations. Proteins can either be complete or incomplete. Complete proteins contain all the essential amino acids, whereas incomplete proteins do not. Obviously, you should shoot for as many complete proteins as possible. For instance, try combining two incomplete proteins (such as rice and beans) to make a meal that has complete protein.

Good places to get protein are through meat, cheese, tofu/soy products, eggs, grains, and some leafy green vegetables. Protein shakes are available, but that's kind of like melting a few different pieces of Lego together to make a new shape—it works, but it's probably not the best idea. Proteins can occasionally be converted into energy through a process known as gluconeogenesis, but this only happens when your body is in starvation mode (as we discussed earlier in the carbohydrate section).

So those form the macronutrients—the major constituents of the food you eat. Now we move on to vitamins and minerals, the micronutrients. You don't need much of them, but you certainly can't do without them. There are some that are called "macrominerals", as you need far more of them than the others on a relative scale. These would be things such as calcium, magnesium, potassium, and sodium.

So that's the theory behind nutrition, but what about it in practice? We have to eat, how do you eat well? The trick is balance—it is my opinion that you can safely disregard any diet that tells you to completely cut something out of your diet, and any diet that tells you to eat excessive quantities of something. This is a general rule with some exceptions, but I hope that you understand the point I'm trying to make—eat a little bit of everything, and not too much of any one thing. If you eat nothing but steaks all day every day, that's fairly unhealthy. But if you eat nothing but tomatoes all day every day, you probably won't do well on that diet either.

Many campuses have recognized the need for their students to eat healthier. After all, well-fed students do better in class, so you can pass, get your degree, and go away faster! I kid, partially, but the institutions do realize the value of nutritious food, and some have even gone so far as to hire a campus nutritionist. At Saint Mary's we have a nutritionist that occasionally runs classes on healthy eating, and these have been well-received by the students. Explore your nutritional options, and you'll find what's right for you.

Confession time: I actually lost fifteen pounds my first year. I know I was supposed to gain fifteen pounds (the much touted "Freshman 15", as it were), but nobody told me that I was supposed to gain weight and so I ended up losing it. A lot of it was due to the fact that I hardly ate in my first month at university, and was stressed to the point of near collapse, but eating well and exercising is what kept the weight off after I started to enjoy myself.

How you eat will largely depend on your living situation: residence dining halls present an entirely different nutritional challenge than cooking your own meals. We'll tackle both, one at a time. First, dining halls. Two methods of food dispersion seem to be the most popular: unlimited food for a limited number of meals per week, or a declining balance system similar to a gift card.

I've eaten under both plans, as I started at Saint Mary's with a declining balance system, but this year the dining hall was transitioned to the more traditional meals per week system. It's been quite the adjustment—I ate until I was nearly sick the first three times I went there, it's just in my nature to want to get as much as I possibly can. I've started getting better at controlling myself recently, though.

What's been the most interesting is how the switch affected my attitudes towards food. If I can delve into a bit of economics, it's changed the opportunity cost of having a meal. Before, food mostly cost money, since I could take it with me wherever I wanted, but it came off my balance. Now, I've paid a set amount of money, in return I get unlimited food whenever I want, but I have to eat it within the walls of the dining hall. This means that food now costs me time rather than money, which has flipped everything on its head.

The trick to eating well in a dining hall environment is to know what you like, know what's good for you, and stick to that. However, this can take a bit of experimentation, so allow yourself a bit of time to become acclimated to the food on offer. Dining halls normally operate on a rotating set of menus that repeat every number of weeks. In time, you'll recognize what's good, what's bad, and what's ugly (like that mystery meat sandwich they offer on Tuesdays).

Take advantage of the salad bar, it's an easy way to get more veggies into your day. It's also a great way to be creative! Stack lettuce and tomatoes to the sky, bolstered by girders of carrot sticks and bolts of celery and green pepper. If you like dressing, go ahead, but go lightly—vegetables have a delicious taste and crunch all their own, which can sometimes be smothered by too much dressing.

How about all you off-campus students? Time can be tight—there are readings to be done, jobs to be worked, assignments to be completed, keggers to be attended, it doesn't leave a lot of time for culinary art to happen. But it's an important thing to learn. An old quote says, "Those who do not make time for health now will have to make time for sickness later". Think about that the next time you're micro-waving a pizza.

But there are times when you genuinely won't have time to cook. Take the start of school, for example. During the writing of this book, I had a period from late August to early September where I didn't write a word for three solid weeks. If I had a minute of spare time, it either went to re-laxing so I'd have energy for the next activity, or to sleeping so I wouldn't drop dead in the hall the next day. I know what it's like to be busy.

So how can you survive during those trying times? Ingenuity is the key. If you're making supper for yourself, make twice as much and take the leftovers for lunch the next day. Note: leftovers don't have to be the same dish—you can build an entirely new second meal out of them, us-ing the leftovers as your base. Make a double batch of pasta, and two different sauces! Instant variety.

Some people take this to extremes in a process known as OAMC, or Once A Month Cooking. In it, they block off a weekend or other continuous set of time to do nothing but cook. And cook they do, preparing a month's worth of food in one shot. There are several different methods to do this by, but the most common way is to make unreasonably large batches of staple foods (pasta, rice, beans, etc.) and freeze them. Then you can have a plethora of different meal combinations throughout the month.

For a more realistic approach, try OAWS—Once A Week Shopping. I don't know if that's an actual program or not, but it's a good idea none-theless. The easiest way to cook tasty meals on a budget is to plan your meals in advance. Some might say that this takes away from the spon-taneity of cooking whatever comes into your head, but I would argue that it not only encourages you to be creative and come up with amazing dishes, but it gives you something to look forward to if you know you have a delicious meal planned for that evening.

Here's one that applies to both dining halls and at home, and I know you've probably heard it ten thousand times before, but eat breakfast. Se-riously, do it. Try a few different cereals, find one you like, and have a bowl of it every morning. Or get a blender, some fruits and yogurt, and make a smoothie. In time it'll just be another part of your morning rou-tine, and not only will it taste great and make you feel better, you'll do better in classes and lose weight too!

Consider this—if you don't eat breakfast, you'll be starving by lunch. And it's all too easy to overeat when you're exceptionally hungry. So eat breakfast, and you'll watch your grades go up while your weight goes down. You don't even need to wait—start tomorrow! You'll see results immediately, and over time. It is the simplest, easiest, and most fun way to improve your life instantaneously.

Anyway, you could write a book on how to eat well, and thousands of people have. This chapter simply aims to give you a good start on healthy eating, under the principles of balance and moderation. Most books try to scare you away from certain foods and promote certain foods, but in the end, it's all food, eaten for the same purpose. Use your common sense, switch out fries for a salad once in a while, and you'll do fine.

Chapter Nine

Presentations:
From Brain To Blackboard

I f you're in university, you are going to have to do presentations. For business students they might be case analyses, in science you'll show off lab reports, arts students have oral exams. I'm obviously generalizing, but my point is that public speaking is a part of university life, and a part of life in general. So why not be better than everyone else at it?

Part of the reason you picked up this book is likely because you want to be better at university than anyone else. So you have the right mindset to become good at this, all it takes is a little training. Here, we'll go over how to make compelling presentations, and how to deliver them well.

The most important part of a speech is the rehearsal. Again: the most important part of a speech is the rehearsal. Three times: the most important part of a speech is the rehearsal. You need to have the text of your speech carved into the base of your skull by the time you're done practicing. However, that doesn't mean you have to remember it all.

In fact, if that were the case you could just read from a paper you wrote. And that would be very boring. No offence, I'm sure your writing is excellent, but there's a very big difference between writing on paper and talking, even when they're on the same subject. When I say rehearsal is important, what I mean is that you should know the topics you're going to discuss forwards, backwards, and upside down dangling over a volcano.

The words are essentially fungible. Economics tip: "fungible" means a commodity that is interchangeable with any other unit of the commodity. Take a litre of milk. Is it any different from any other litre of milk? No. So in your speech, the words you use to talk about your ideas are secondary to the ideas that you attempt to convey.

However, there are no absolutes in this chapter. Sometimes, the words you use to talk about your ideas are VERY important, and in these times you should memorize down to the letter what you are going to say. But more often than not it doesn't matter what the individual words are, but what you are trying to convey.

"This is my son, mine own Telemachus, to whom I leave the scepter and the isle. Well-loved of me, discerning to fulfill this labour, by slow prudence to make mild a rugged people, and thro' soft degrees subdue them to the useful and the good. Most blameless is he, centred in the sphere of common duties, decent not to fail in offices of tenderness, and pay meet adoration to my household gods, when I am gone. He works his work, I mine."

- Leaving scepter and isle to son Telemachus
- Believes he will do a good job
  o He's a bit dull, but then so is the job
  o Will likely do fine

Now if you were going to make a speech, which one of those two up there would you find easier to memorize? The second one, of course. If you wanted to, you could certainly memorize the first one, and it would be great, but it would take a long time and there's always the chance that you would go blank in front of the crowd. By keeping what you're really trying to get across in mind, you'll come across as a much more effective speaker.

This really is the key to being an effective speaker. How I memorize a speech is similar to my note-taking style: I start with the full text of what I want to say, and create an outline from that. Then I study that outline until I can deliver the full speech by reading it. Then I summarize the speech further and further until I can do five minutes of speaking off of a single bullet point.

Then practice the speech from memory. And this is where the rehearsal truly comes in handy. Practice your speech wherever you are. Practice it on the treadmill. Practice it when you're in bed awake at night. Practice it waiting for elevators, or in the lunch line. It doesn't have to be out loud, just get comfortable with the way the words work together, and how the speech flows.

As the day draws near, assemble a group of trusted friends to act as your audience. This could be as small as one person, the important part is that you are doing the speech, out loud, from memory, to another human being. If you can talk to one person, why not five? If five, why not fifteen? If fifteen, why not fifty? And so on. The largest speech I've ever given was to over three hundred people at my high school, but I didn't notice any difference in nervousness from when I gave the same speech to an audience of five. The biggest leap in nerves comes going from zero people to one person, so if you can get over that you'll be fine.

People think that if they rehearse too much, they'll look over-rehearsed. I would like to say that there is no such thing, and that those people are just making excuses to be lazy. If you repeat the same words over and over and over again ten times, you probably will be sounding pretty flat by the tenth time. So it would seem to me that maybe you shouldn't focus so much on the words, and instead on the meaning.

People say "Stick to the script. Do not deviate from the script." And that's good advice. But I interpret it a bit differently than most. For me, it means that you should talk about everything you want to talk about, and nothing you don't. If you are a Prime Minister, President, Supreme Court Justice, or any other person whose words are going to be painstakingly analyzed, a prepared statement may be the best option. If you are a news anchor or call centre employee, and your script has been prepared by professional writers, then sticking to the script is the right choice. But otherwise, getting the idea across is much more important than the words you use to get there.

Hand gestures are important, but they can backfire. Think back to commercials or speeches you've seen where people have clearly been told "move your hands like this at this point…. then like this…. then like this." It comes off looking disturbing and robotic. The easiest way to have natural-looking hand gestures is to speak about something you're passionate about.

Think of your hands as punctuation. When you make a point that you really want to stand out, gesture to make that happen. To illustrate the relationship between your two points, gesture to make that happen. You have two hands, so perhaps one hand represents one point, one hand represents the other. Maybe you draw in the air in front of you to show a quick graph you're talking about. The key is to make the gestures about the speech, but not of the speech.

Want to know the easiest way to learn how to be a good speaker? Watch speeches. It seems simple, because it is. In my school, we were constantly having people come in to give talks on various topics, most of which I was not interested in. But I studied their speaking style: what did I like the most? What differentiated good speakers from bad speakers, and great speakers from good speakers?

In my experience, the difference is simple: knowledge. A speech is more than just a series of words arranged in grammatical fashion, it's a way of communicating the contents of your brain to the world at large.

And that's an amazingly powerful thing. Read everything you can get your hands on about public speaking—an astonishing amount of books and online resources are available to teach you how to give a proper presentation, check some of them out.

So your speech flows beautifully from A to Z, you know what you want to cover, you have a good idea of how you're going to cover it, and then you've rehearsed it out to crazy extents. Now comes the easier part—making the slideshow. Or at least, it should be the easier part. People screw up slideshows a lot.

Rule #1: It is a slide, not a book. People can read faster than you can talk, so if all the information is up there on the slide, your speech isn't adding anything, it's slowing things down. The key to a good presentation is simplicity.

Say you're making a presentation about the structure of a caffeine molecule. You have two choices for this presentation: you can copy and paste something from your chemistry textbook up onto the slide, and read it, or you can have a picture of a caffeine molecule, talk about how it's structured, and refer to the picture as necessary.

I've had profs who have done both. One makes me wonder about molecular structure, and one makes me wonder about the likelihood of my glasses breaking if I passed out and my head hit the desk in front of me.

The quick rule of thumb is this: if you can remove it from the slide, you should. Put as much into your speech as you can, and put the highlights up on screen to keep people on track as to what you're talking about. This makes note-taking much easier.

So that's pretty much it for presentations. Be passionate, be concise, and rehearse one hour for every minute of actual speaking time.

Chapter Ten

Team Skills:
Why Can't We All Just
Get Along?

If there's one thing you'll have a lot of in university, it's fun. But if there are two things you'll have a lot of in university, they are fun and team projects. At times, large portions of your grade will be determined by not how smart you are, but by how smart your classmates are. Before you run off screaming, read this portion of the book; it's dedicated to helping you survive and thrive in a team atmosphere.

What are some of the advantages of working in a team? Well, there's the old saying "two heads are better than one", and that is largely true— if you have two people working on a problem, you are likely to come up with more possible solutions, increasing the chances of finding the best one. It also allows your prof to assign bigger projects, as they assume you'll be spreading the work out equally.

In addition, having a group of people on a team ensures that a wide range of knowledge can be covered—perhaps you're very good at economics, your first teammate is very good at accounting, and your second teammate is excellent at marketing. This allows you to tackle a much wider spread of problems than if each of you were to go out on your own.

And finally, there's the motivation of being on a team—nobody wants to be the slowest one, or the one who doesn't contribute; everyone wants to impress their teammates, so this can act as a powerful motivating factor when people are placed in a team environment.

However, not every team is perfect. Some people have no problem being thought of as slow, some people don't really care what the end result of the team project is. If it were up to you, I know you'd choose to boot these people off of your team in favour of people who actually want to be there, but if you tell your prof or TA this they'll probably just say that it "simulates a real-world work environment" or some other line.

They may be right, but it can still be tricky having a bad team. How can you fix this? Let's go back to the beginning, back to when you were first assigned the project. You need to meet soon after the project is assigned, and start dividing up tasks. Then write down what each person is

101

responsible for, and send a copy to your prof or TA. Hopefully this will motivate people to do what they say they will.

Then, people disperse. Meet up a week later and see how people are coming along. If someone is ahead of where they thought they'd be, congratulate them! If someone is lagging behind, investigate why before immediately blaming them—maybe they have a tough course load, or family issues. However, gently remind them that they still need to get the work done on time, as other people are counting on them.

As the work slowly gets done, people will start to feel better as they start to see it coming together. As the due date draws near, keep checking in with people, and meet up beforehand to bring the whole effort together into one piece. How you do this will depend on what kind of group project it is.

If it's a paper, read all the parts together to see if they fit, and edit them as necessary. It's like putting together a few different pieces of wood: they may be different heights and types and you need to sand them a bit in order for everything to look smooth. If you're doing a group presentation, then you need to PRACTICE. A lot.

Seriously, I've already written a chapter on this, but I cannot emphasize it enough. If you're doing a group presentation, then you need to research it, create it, then practice it until your jaw wants to fall off.

Hopefully, by the end you've put together a great piece of work, and it gets a great mark. But that may not always be the case. And that is where the peer evaluation form comes in. At the end of the project, your prof will hand them out to everyone, and ask you for your opinion on how each member of your team did.

If you had a team of four, this could range from ranking them one to four, dividing up four hundred points between them, or any number of other odd strategies. One of the more interesting ways I've seen this done is that you split up percentages between your team members, and then those percentages are summed up, and your final mark gets multiplied by it.

It's a bit odd to explain without actual numbers, so imagine that your paper, for whatever reason, got a mark of 56. You are obviously terrified that this is going to negatively impact your grade. However, your teammates think you did well on the paper compared to others, so their peer evaluations of you are 30 percent, 27 percent, 40 percent, and 26 percent. So your final mark is multiplied by 30+27+40+26 = 123 percent. Lucky you.

Note: when you get your evaluation form, most of your team members will simply give everyone 25 percent and hand it back immediately without thinking. They will likely pressure you to do the same. I would ask you to consider how many times you've been on a team where everyone contributed absolutely equally. It's happened to me, but it certainly doesn't happen every time. So I would encourage you to think hard about what each person contributed, and mark accordingly.

Now I'm going to lay some theory on you. It's called the Four Stages of Team Development. They are: Forming, Storming, Norming, and Performing. I know, these management theoreticians just think they're so clever, don't they?

Forming is the first stage, where the team comes together. Maybe you'll get to pick your group, but probably you won't. This is because profs know you'll only get into groups with your friends, and they want you to "be diverse" and "challenge your expectations". So just deal with it, and try to make some new friends. Who knows, maybe you'll get lucky and be on a team with at least one person you know.

In the Forming stage, you should concentrate on setting expectations and goals for your team—how often are you going to meet, who is going to work on what, when do the pieces need to be done so you can bring it together into one piece? A little bit of writing things down now can save a lot of arguing later on. Also, if you have any great research resources, or you know a lot about the subject the project's on, now would be a good time to reveal this information.

The next part is Storming. You'll know when you reach this stage, trust me. This is where things start to turn ugly, people start slacking on work, and divisions occur between team members. Everyone thinks that they are the sole voice of truth and reason on the team, destined to save the others from themselves. This can be harsh for a team, but it can also make you stronger.

The Storming stage is so important to team development because it's where your best ideas may come from. Knocking the stuffing out of each other nullifies weak ideas and allows the good ones to rise to the surface. Or at least that's how it's supposed to work. If you end up with a group that does nothing but argue with one another, that may be a bit tricky.

You see, there's a fine line between "constructive criticism" and "telling someone how much you hate their work". A team whose members feel that they are not allowed to criticize decisions will not move forward, but a team that spends all its time mired in endless debate will be frozen just the same. Tolerance and patience are key in this segment, if the team is ever to move on to the Norming stage.

In Norming, the team has gone through its troubles and fused itself together as one. You begin to see each other as true colleagues and teammates, and productivity rises. However, you still need to keep an eye out for when your team is running "too smoothly". This can be a sign that people are afraid to rock the boat now that things are going well, and it needs to be stamped out. When a team of four begins to think as one, it loses three other brains.

If your team is truly lucky, you'll reach the Performing stage. This is where everything starts to click—your teammates are good at their jobs, you're good at yours, the work is going off with mechanical precision, and people are comfortable speaking up if something's not going quite right. Workers are largely independent, and team leaders serve more as guides than managers.

A good example of this would be a car factory—if you're fitting car parts on an American assembly line, it works this way: put the part on, and if it doesn't fit, throw it out and try another one. In Japan, every worker has the power to shut down the entire line to fix a problem. They want to know why the part doesn't fit. That way, problems can be fixed, and waste is minimized.

So now that your team has gone through all the different stages, you're done, right? Unfortunately, no. Team dynamics are a constantly changing medium, and changes may lead to the team falling back to any of the previous stages. If a new team member joins, you have to teach them how to work according to the rules of the team, which sets you back into Norming, for example.

So that's a really academic explanation of what will happen to you when you inevitably form into teams in your classes. The simple, short version of it is:

- You'll get shoved in a group with a bunch of people you don't know.
- You'll gradually get to know them.
- You'll fight with them a lot.
- You'll eventually stop fighting and actually get to work.
- You'll slowly become a better and better team.
- And then it'll all be over.

Chapter Eleven

You Need Sleep.
Trust Me, You Do.

A h, sleep. Lay down in a nice warm bed and shut off your mind for a few hours while you rest. However, in university this magical time can be delayed much further than it should be. Perhaps you do it on purpose, perhaps it's just due to nerves. This chapter is dedicated to helping you get the rest you need to be at your best.

What is sleep, really? You can break it down into two parts—REM sleep, or "Rapid Eye Movement" sleep, and NREM sleep, or "Non-Rapid Eye Movement Sleep". Those two categories pretty much cover the whole thing. In REM sleep, your eyes jump around a lot, your brain displays high levels of activity, and your muscles are largely paralyzed to prevent you from flailing about too much.

Why would you flail about? It's because REM sleep is when dreaming happens. So if you dream about chasing a bus that never gets any nearer, it prevents you from running into a wall. REM sleep normally occupies about 25-30 percent of your total sleep time, coming in short bursts about four or five times per night. There are some theories that say that REM sleep is when your memories are consolidated, which makes sense.

Non-REM sleep is, understandably, all the parts of your sleep that aren't REM sleep. It's divided into three stages, with gradually declining brain activity in each stage. However, there is no eye movement, little to no dreaming, and your muscles are not paralyzed, as in REM sleep. How you feel upon waking up is largely dependent on when you're woken up in your sleep cycle.

For instance, if you're woken up during REM sleep, or the final stage of NREM sleep, studies have shown that you can experience mental slowness for up to thirty minutes after awakening. You've probably already experienced this: I know from my own experience that some mornings I wake up feeling great and some mornings I.... well, let's just say some mornings I don't wake up feeling great, and leave it at that.

Interesting fact: there is a sleep disorder known as "exploding head syndrome". I am not kidding. It doesn't have to do with needing to pick up brain fragments off your pillow in the morning, it simply consists of an enormously loud noise emanating seemingly from within the head of the person affected, during the mid-stages of NREM. It isn't physically harmful, but can be a bit disturbing.

So how much sleep should you get? Well that depends on a case by case basis, but try to shoot for around seven hours per night. If you have an 8:30 class, you could sleep from 1 am to 8 am, and bring breakfast to class with you, like I did in my second year. Over time, you'll find what works for you, depending on how much you need to get done, and when you need to do it.

If your schedule is completely flexible, you could try experimenting with a polyphasic sleep schedule. This is where instead of one large chunk of sleep per day, you sleep several times per day for shorter periods of time. More information is available online if you're interested in pursuing this, but this book will mostly focus on a monophasic sleep schedule, as it is what I have the most experience with.

Think of how much you sleep each night. Is it enough? Why or why not? If you get into bed but have trouble falling asleep, try using some of that tossing and turning time to consider your day up to that point. Were you running around all day until you collapsed into bed? If so, it's only natural for your body to require time to wind down and relax.

Try instituting a bedtime ritual to let your body know you're getting ready to go to bed—for instance, when I'm getting ready to go to bed I'll turn out most of the lights in my room, stretch out in a comfy chair, and watch some TV to calm my mind down from the day. Try to avoid horror movies, or complex documentaries, as these will likely be counterproductive to your goal of relaxation.

But sometimes you just can't seem to get to sleep. I've been there, I know how frustrating it can be. I remember back in my first year, I laid in bed for eight straight hours the night before my first ever university exam, and I was panicking that I was going to be overtired for the exam, and fail the course, and everyone would laugh at me, and my life would be over. Like I said, I was a weird kid my first semester at university.

And then something else weird happened: nothing. I went in, and wasn't tired. I ended up getting one of the highest marks in my class on the exam, and it taught me a valuable lesson about stressing out too much about sleep. Granted, there are things you can do to sleep better, but there are times when your body will simply have other ideas. Accept those times, and work with them.

Two common artificial methods of falling asleep that are widely used are alcohol and sleeping pills. I can't in good conscience recommend either. Sleeping pills seem like a great fix at the time, but they can become addictive, and less effective over time. In addition, they can contain some pretty heavy medical tranquilizers, which make you unconscious, but not really "asleep". Not to mention what might happen if you really needed to be awake for a good reason (fire, violent intruder, etc.)

That said, far be it from me to contradict the opinions of your medical professional. If they say you should do it, it's probably a good idea. Just make sure to be careful about it. Alcohol is another common treatment for insomnia, with troubling results. Now it is true that alcohol is a depressant, and after a beer or two you may feel like you're tired, but it doesn't last.

Not only does it act like a diuretic and make you have to make a midnight bathroom run, but its second-stage effects stimulate the body and make it harder to get back to sleep. The easiest way to fall asleep is through simple relaxation techniques. Go through your day in detail in your mind: what did you do that day? Start with what you had for breakfast, and you'll likely be out by the time you hit lunch.

However, we don't live in a perfect world. And that's why I am going to teach you how to sleep in class. Disclaimer: this should not be done on a regular basis, it is a last-ditch solution at best.

It starts with your clothing, in that it shouldn't be overly attention-grabbing. If the reason you need sleep is that you're still in last night's bar attire, your problems might be a bit different than the ones this book was designed to handle.

Dress in greys and wear a hat, if your professor is alright with them. Sit in the middle of the class, not so far forward that you call attention to yourself, but not so far back that it's blatantly obvious you're sleeping. Don't put your head down, rest your chin in the space between your thumb and index finger. There—you look deep in thought, with your eyes closed to absorb the material better. Now try not to let it happen again, eh?

To sum up, sleep is important. Duh. But it's not always easy to get—so make sure to maximize your REM and late-stage NREM sleep, start instituting a bedtime routine to relax at the end of the day, and try to not drug yourself to sleep, it'll hurt you in the long run. One last tip: your prof will often summarize their lecture at the end, in a form sort of like this, so try to wake up a few minutes before class ends to catch that part. This will also prevent you from being the one who got caught sleeping in class because they were still pretending to write ten minutes after the prof stopped talking. Sweet dreams!

Appendices

Appendix A – How To Play The Three Most Popular Drinking Games

Alright. So you're going to university. There will be drinking. Just do it legally, and do it responsibly. Everything you read in this part of the book should only be applied if you are the legal drinking age in your area.

That said, there are three main drinking games played on every university campus on the continent: Beer Pong, Quarters, and Flip Cup. In this section, I will take you through each game, describe how it's played, and how you can beat your friends at it.

Beer Pong

In ancient Greece, they played a game called Kottabos, where philosophers would take whatever was left over in the bottom of their wine glasses, and hurl it at a target. Socrates was rumoured to be quite the skilled player. Nowadays we have Beer Pong. The undisputed champion of irresponsible campus behaviour, Wikipedia lists the skills required to play as, "aiming, taunting, and alcohol tolerance". It's also known as Beirut on some campuses.

There are "official" rules, but here's a fairly simple setup:

1. Acquire a table, about the same size as a ping pong table.
2. Set up the cups
   a. Six or ten cups per side, pyramid formation with rims touching, one inch from the table's back edge.
3. Pour an agreed-upon amount of alcohol into each cup.
   a. In total, aim to use about two beers, one per team member.
   b. If you're using standard plastic cups, the first inside ridge is usually used.
4. Take turns throwing a ping pong ball across the table and attempting to land it in one of the other team's cups. If you hit, they drink. If your teammate also hits, you get an extra shot.

113

5. Reset the cups into a pyramid at intervals of six, three, and one.

6. The losing team is the first one to run out of cups.

One popular house rule is the "Babe Ruth Rule". Essentially, it says that before you throw, you can call which cup you're going to sink it into, and if it goes in that cup, it's worth two drinks. However, if you miss, you have to drink one of your own cups. Only you can decide if that's a risk worth taking.

There are three main tosses: the arc, the bounce, and the fastball (or "laser"). The arc is the most common shot, performed by grasping the ball with the thumb and two fingers and then throwing with the bicep parallel to the table.

More aggressive players may opt for the fastball, where the ball is whipped at the opposing team's cup with the intention of knocking it over. The popularity of this toss depends on house rules, as not all games dictate that an overturned cup counts as being eliminated.

The final common throw is the bounce shot, where the player aims to hit the table halfway and then have the ball bounce up into one of the cups. Again, this throw is dependent on house rules, as they may specify that players are allowed to swat away balls that have already hit the table. Be a showoff at your own risk.

Quarters

Quarters is one of the old-school drinking games, the one your dad probably played (whether he wants to tell you or not). Like Beer Pong, it also has a fairly simplistic premise:

1. Get a table.
   a. Put a tablecloth on it to avoid denting the table, while still retaining bounce.
2. Put a glass in the middle.
   a. You can either pre-fill it with beer, or have everyone drink from their own glass.
   b. The size will vary depending on your skill, from rocks glasses to shot glasses.
3. Get a quarter.
   a. You can hold it by the edge or the face, your choice.
4. Bring your arm down onto the table, and (hopefully) bounce the quarter into the glass.

a. If you sink it, choose someone to drink it. If you miss, pass it on.

Flip Cup

This is the game you break out when you have a lot of people, who all want to drink right now. This game can be played with (theoretically) any number of people, as long as you have at least four. According to Wikipedia, the skills required for Flip Cup are "cup-flipping and beer-chugging". Again, a simple setup:

1. Get a table.
2. Have people form equal lines on each side of the table.
3. Put cups on the table, as many as there are people playing.
4. Fill the cups with a standard measure of beer.
    a. Again, the first ridge on a normal plastic cup is fairly universal.
5. The first two people in line touch cups, drink, and then place their cup back on the table so its bottom slightly overhangs the edge.
6. They then attempt to flip the cup (hence the name) so that the rim lands and sticks upside down on the table.
a. As with golf or any sport, a good follow-through is key to success.
b. Sprinkling a bit of beer on the table beforehand can help it stick, if you're just starting.
    7. When the first person has successfully flipped their cup, the second person in line drinks.
    8. Repeat steps five through seven until there is nobody left. The first team to finish is the winner!

Possible variations include:
• Jungle Rules
    o Everyone drinks at the same time, and the first side to finish and flip all their cups wins.
• Survivor Flip Cup
    o The losing team must vote off a member and have someone drink two cups next time.
• KOT (King of the Table)
    o Everyone drinks and flips at the same time, last person to finish is eliminated.
    o Progresses onward until only one person is left.

If someone disputes your interpretation of the rules, try and work things out calmly. Four days before I wrote this, a game of Flip Cup in Montana turned ugly, and ended with a man stabbing his friend in the stomach and nearly murdering him. So always remember to play nice, ok?

The Requisite Serious Part

Like I said before, if you're smart enough to get into university, you're smart enough that I shouldn't need to tell you that binge drinking is bad for you, and that you shouldn't drink and drive. Someone dies every forty seconds from drinking and driving. Don't let it be you, and certainly don't let it be because of you.

For Beer Pong, you should wash your hands before touching anything that's about to be flung into a cup of beer. Trust me, alcohol kind of loses its germ-killing power when you mix it with barley and hops. And if you want to be overly safe, these games are just as much fun if you don't play with beer. You can certainly drink if you want, but I've had great times playing with water. Plus, as a bonus, your aim doesn't suffer as much.

But at every party, there will be someone who doesn't listen. Someone who decides to go just a round or two too far with the drinking. This next section will help you to help them.

When you realize that someone is drunk (slurred speech, an odd approach to walking, maybe they try to ride the beer pong table like it's a horse), then you should step in and try to help. Get them some air, maybe convince them to pack things in. If nothing else, offer to buy them a rum and cola and come back with just cola.

They need to get home, and many times you'll be faced with two choices: walking, or a cab. Some fresh air and brisk exercise can be just what your average drunkard needs to wake up their system, but some people are the types who decide to use the middle of the road as a restroom, or pick a fight with a pigeon because it "looked at him funny". In this case, a cab may be the easiest and safest way to get home.

Just make sure they have the window open, and remember (here's a tip for the physics majors) that it's impossible to vomit out of the window of a moving car, the air currents will simply blow the vomit back in your face. Ensure that the cab driver knows he may have to make an urgent stop at some point.

If, despite your efforts, they end up, ahem, "making a call on the porcelain telephone", then when you get home and put them to bed you should put them in the recovery position, and make sure their airway is clear. This will prevent them from choking on their own vomit, which is one of the lesser dignified ways one can die. However, you should never induce vomiting in someone who is intoxicated, it will not make them better.

To put someone in the recovery position, roll them onto their side, with one knee raised to prevent them from rolling. Once they're there, stick around with them to make sure they keep breathing during the night. Alcohol poisoning, which is denoted by blue lips, a rapid pulse, clammy hands/feet, and being short of breath, kills university students every year, and it's a shame.

If you think that your friend might be in trouble, don't panic, just call 911 and explain the situation. I don't care if they're underage. Do you want them to live or not? It's a simple choice. Make sure they stay alive, and everything else will work itself out in time.

Appendix B - Four Ways To Open A Bottle Without A Bottle Opener

$5 bill – Five dollars will get you a drink or two, depending on where and when you're buying. But how do you actually translate money into an open beer? Simple. Take the bill, fold it in half. Now roll it up, and fold it in half again. It'll be trickier the second time, and you probably won't be able to fold it completely over.

Instead, you'll end up with a V-shaped object, which you then wedge the point of up under the cap. Grip the neck of the beer firmly in one hand, press up on the bill with the other, and watch the cap soar across the room.

Another beer - There are times at university when you will only have one beer lying around, but hopefully this isn't one of them, since this method of opening a bottle requires a second bottle. Set the bottle you want to open on a table or other sturdy surface, and find the ridge halfway up the cap on the bottle you want to use as your opener.

Then, use this ridge to slowly pry off the top of your second bottle. Note: make sure you use the ridge, and not the cap itself. Otherwise, you run the risk of not knowing which cap is going to give way first. And that's a very messy risk to take.

A lighter – Cigarettes are bad for you. But then again, so is drinking, and yet here we are. People don't always make the healthy choice, but this time you can benefit from it. The science-major way of doing this would be to light the lighter, use it to soften the metal of the cap, and then pry it off before it hardens.

You could certainly do that, but it's been my experience that mixing fire and alcohol usually ends badly. So how can you get an open beer without the risk of an open flame? Use the other end of the lighter. It has a solid plastic bottom which is perfect for gradually easing the cap up off of the neck.

A key – The key to your residence room could also be the key to your future intoxication. Examine the bumps on the key. Find one that's long, and isolated, and wedge it up under one of the crimps on the cap. Then repeat this step a few times on neighboring crimps until you've bent up about 1/3 of the cap. Then you can fit the key into the hole, and by pressing upwards you can unlock the beer.

So there you have it, four ways to open a bottle without an opener. Just remember one next time, will you?

Appendix C – The Original Facebook Note

Yes, it's hard to imagine that this all started with a couple of random paragraphs that I jotted down and decided to post online. But here they are, for posterity:

One big thing about university: It's a lot more work.

I know, I know, you've been told this every year about every grade above you. "Grade __ will be a lot more work than now." And it never turns out to be true, does it?

So I went into SMU thinking, "yeah, yeah, yeah, more work, sure, I know."

I DIDN'T KNOW.

It really is a lot more work, I'm completely serious and not kidding at all.

Not to mention you're completely responsible for it—no teachers bugging you and putting due dates up on the board, no parents on your case for being on Facebook.

So find a good place to study (a library is the stereotype for a reason—it works!) and then DO IT!

Other good things:

1) Go to your frosh week events. They're fun, probably free or close to it, and they get you out there.

2) But don't overdo it. I went out to everything for the first three days. By Day Four I had nothing left, and missed out on some cool stuff.

3) You will not make friends overnight—get used to it. Think about high school. How long did it take you to rise to your currently level of fame (or infamy)? Remember that figure when it seems like nobody is noticing you. I went to SMU expecting to make all these instant lifelong friends, and when it didn't happen, I was crushed and thought the problem was me. It's not—people just don't make friends that quickly, especially under university stress levels.

Also, realize: You are not obligated to be friends with anyone, and they are not obligated to befriend you. Your floormates may be great people, or they may be your polar opposites. Be ready.

Want to know the best way to meet friends? Join a society. You'll meet people that you have more in common with than just applying to residence at the same time, or signing up for the same course.

4) EAT. Food keeps your body and mind at their best, and you need them that way. When I first got to SMU, I was so nervous I didn't eat for a week. In retrospect, not eating probably messed me up more than anything else—your body needs food. And try to eat healthy—I know you're away from home and can eat pizza three meals a day if you want, but does that mean you have to? No.

If you're like me and literally can't eat, drink. Apple juice, milk, protein shakes, anything to keep your body going. ALCOHOL DOES NOT COUNT! As long as you keep something fueling your body, you'll feel better. Then gradually build up—salads are a great light way of filling yourself up at first, then move to heavier food.

5) Exercise. I simply cannot emphasize how important this is. A rising tide lifts all boats—if you exercise, everything gets better: your mood, your health, your grades.

If you're like me, and taking a study break makes you feel like a slacker, exercise! It's hard to feel like you're not doing anything worthwhile when you know you are.

Don't have time? Make time. Set a textbook on the handlebars of your stationary bike, tape flash cards to the floor of your treadmill, hire someone to put subliminal messages in your exercise tapes, just be creative. It's so important, you can't afford to pass it up.

6) Yes, you made the right choice. If you are motivated and driven enough to decide you want to go to university, then pick one, then jump through all the necessary hoops to get there, you are exactly the type of person who should be there. So stop doubting yourself.

Now, a reality check. It is possible that despite everything, university and you just don't get along. However, THIS HAPPENS A LOT LESS THAN YOU THINK—IT'S VERY UNLIKELY TO BE YOU. But, I just thought I'd throw it out there. If you really think you've screwed up, talk to your academic advisor (or whatever service your university offers).

7) This is the most important one. No matter how bad things get, don't change yourself. If you're not a drinker, don't start just to fit in. Sitting out in a parking lot around someone's car getting wasted may seem like a favourable alternative to going back to your room, but you have to have the mental fortitude and willpower to know whether it REALLY is, or if you just want friends, any friends.

The want to fit in can be a strong motivator, but you have to keep reminding yourself—you're not truly fitting in if you have to change yourself to do it. Fitting a square peg in a round hole is tough, but is it really a victory if you succeed by chopping the corners off?

8) Sleep. I had a roommate first week, because I thought it would be interesting. Oh, and it was. It was so interesting I couldn't sleep. And sleep deprivation is used as torture for a reason—it really screws you up.

So please, for your own sake, take careful consideration of your sleep requirements, and make sure to accommodate them—earplugs, eye masks, a spare sock to jam in your roomie's mouth, bring whatever you think you might need.

I wrote this from the point of view "What would have helped me in my first week?" I hope it helps you.

-Steve

P.S. A lot of schools offer counseling services for students. It can be really nice to go and talk to someone who's not a professor, not a parent, and not a fellow student. So give it a shot. There's really no shame in it.